Diane Robinson Mullins

Gazelle
P R E S S

Groomed to Grow
by Diane Robinson Mullins

ISBN 1-58169-150-5
For Worldwide Distribution
Printed in the U.S.A.

Gazelle Press
P.O. Box 191540 • Mobile, AL 36619
800-367-8203

Table of Contents

Dedication

I lovingly dedicate this book to these precious people who have taught me so much by the lives which they live. They have allowed me to seek the face of God and move into His purpose for my life:

My husband, James H. Mullins, Jr., who since the day we met, has pushed me to be all that God has called me to be. You are the love of my life and the best daddy that our two sons could ever have.

My mother, Nancy Vaughn, who has lived a godly life in front of me and been an example of courage and faith in the midst of trying and fearful times. If it wasn't for you, I wouldn't be where I am now. Thanks, Mom.

My father-in-love, James H. Mullins, Sr., who has truly shown me how to love people and allow His mercy to flow, even when you don't feel like it. I would have messed things up a long time ago if I had not been able to watch you think first, then speak later. Thank you.

My grandmother, Georgia Robinson. Thank you for my dad and all of your prayers. I love you!

And to my Lord and Savior, Jesus Christ, I am Yours. If not for You, life would not be worth living. You give me purpose and life. I love You, and I am eternally Yours.

In Memory

In loving memory of my dad, Pastor Pearl Robinson, who taught me by example and by his fiery sermons of the truth of the Word. The foundations I base my life upon are those he taught as I watched and listened.

My precious mother-in-love, Pat Mullins. Her prophetic insight into the move of God and also into the lives of the people she pastored, caused me to seek the face of the Lord to know Him as she did.

Acknowledgments

To my sons, Cody and Jordan, for understanding and patience during the times that I have to be away. I love you both very much. You are special young men!

Kathy Halderman for your typing and proofreading and taking the time to listen, during the good and the bad times. I truly love and appreciate you.

Sherrie Neal for all the proofreading and creative ideas. I love you and appreciate your God-given ability with words.

Gene Vaughn, my stepfather, for all the times you give Mom up to let her be with me. Thank you for your love and understanding.

To my church family of Calvary Christian Center, I say thank you for allowing me to study and teach, and sometimes stumble, and always loving me, encouraging me to reach for the best! I love all of you!

Introduction

Purpose—the very word frightens some and excites others. No matter what emotion we feel when we hear the word, we all have to be prepared to fulfill our divine purpose in life.

I have dreamed big dreams and made big plans throughout my life. Many times I have thought I was ready to conquer the world, just to find out I wasn't ready at all. Zeal without knowledge and gifts without character landed me flat on my face. I had many rough edges that had to be smoothed out.

In Psalm 139 David refers to a book that God had written about his life and his days before he had lived any of them. If God penned a book about David's life, then He has written concerning our days as well. I have often wondered how closely the way I have lived my life parallels the plan that God recorded before I was born.

Every person has been given a divine destiny, no matter where we are from or what our place in life is. Life is all a matter of the choices we make. The greatest power on earth is the power of man's will. Our heavenly Father, the divine Creator, presents us with choices every day. How and what we choose directly affects who we are and what we accomplish in our lives.

Joshua found the key to fulfilling his purpose in life. He realized early on that he had to first learn to closely follow his appointed leader, Moses. In studying the life of Joshua, we see that he was being groomed to take Moses' place to lead the children of Israel into their promised land. He was with Moses when he went up to the mountain of the Lord. He waited on Moses for 40 days and 40 nights, alone and cold, not really understanding what was going on. He was able to face the darkness of each night because the man of God told him to wait. He was obedient and didn't walk away from difficulty because he simply felt like it. He was with Moses when he came down out of the mountain. He witnessed the glory of the Lord upon him!

When Moses left the tent of meeting and went inside the camp of Israel, Joshua stayed by himself in the presence of the Lord. He learned to linger there, alone, in God's glorious presence. Through Moses' example, he learned where to find his help and his direction.

He desired to know the Lord, to hear His voice and His command, but to fulfill his destiny he needed to grow. He had to change. He became willing, whatever the cost, to endure whatever it took to be all that God had called him to be.

Today God is calling us to come up to the mountain. He is drawing us to the place of intimacy with Himself. He bids us to wait in His presence, yielding to the changes that need to be made. We must allow the cutting away of the flesh, those areas in us that are unlike Him.

All experiences have to be walked out every day that we live. It is time to quit walking around the same mountain, day after day, with no success, no change, and no growth. We have to grow up. There are no shortcuts. Obedience to God is the path we must follow. There is a destiny to be fulfilled and an inheritance to possess.

Joshua's life is filled with examples of triumph and tragedy, trials and victory, joy and pain. We can learn many principles by the life that he lived. Like Joshua, we must go through the process. Our heavenly Father is grooming us to grow…

My prayer is the following song the Lord gave me:

Pliable

On the center of the anvil
My life has been laid,
As the hammer of the Spirit
Reshapes mistakes I've made.
I don't always like it
But I know it has to be,
That the character of Jesus
May be seen in me.

I will be pliable
In Your hands, Lord,
I will not reply against thee
Though sometimes it seems the pressure
Is more than I can stand.
I will be pliable
In Your hand.

With singleness of vision
I can finally see,
Though I must admit
Your forming hand
Brings me to my knees.
Endurance is the answer
Lord, help me to withstand.
Conform me to Your image
For I know this is Your plan.

CHAPTER ONE

DIVINE PURPOSE

Each of us, regardless of talent, ability, looks, possessions (or lack of), has been given a purpose, a divine destiny to fulfill while we live here on earth. God Himself, our Master Creator, placed His purpose within each one of us before we were born.

Psalms 139:13-16 states

For You formed my inward parts; You covered me in my mother's womb. I will praise You, for I am fearfully and wonderfully made; Marvelous are Your works, My frame was not hidden from You, when I was made in secret, and skillfully wrought in the lowest parts of the earth. Your eyes saw my substance, being yet unformed. And in Your book they were all written, the days fashioned for me, when as yet there were none of them.

God inscribed our days into a book before we ever lived any of them. How would the book you have written, by the life you have lived, compare with the book He has written about you?

I have learned that God uses everything we walk through as a life lesson to teach us principles and character so that He can use us for His glory and for His honor. We will not always understand, but we must learn to hold His "unchanging hand" and never let go and trust Him to lead us on! It is only in the place of your divine purpose that you will find rest and fulfillment.

We need to understand that God's will and His way are the best for us and we must pursue them at the speed of light. Did you know that light travels through space at the speed of 186,000 miles per second? Let's get going—we have already wasted too much precious time!

Psalms 40:8 states "I delight to do thy will O my God, and Your law is within my heart." There is only one thing more important than doing the will of God and that is that we delight to do His will. Obedience to the Lord should be the joy and strength of our life. Delighting to do His will comes through an intimate, personal relationship with the Lord that grows day by day!_

God's will may not always be comfortable to us. Walking in our purpose at times may be uncomfortable, but it must be our delight and heartbeat. His Word should rule in our hearts. No matter what the cost, we need to rejoice in His plan and purpose for our lives.

God created each one of us with a distinct purpose in mind. It is a joy to know that God does not produce any one person in mass quantities.; each of us is distinctively different. God does not create duplicates or carbon copies. I always say, "God has to have a sense of humor, just look at the person in the mirror". When He created us, He threw away the mold, and no one else can as effectively do what we were created to do.

On a table one day, I saw a silver jug with milk in it. A little brown earthen jug was also sitting on the table with rich cream in it. Nobody refused the cream just because it was in an earthen jar. We all love the silver jugs, but God loves to put His richest treasures in the earthen jars.

—ANDREW MURRAY

However, we possess this precious treasure [the divine light of the Gospel] *in* [frail, human] *vessels of earth, that the grandeur and exceeding greatness of the power may be shown to be from God and not from ourselves* (II Corinthians 4:7).

Let's face it. Without the Lord, we *are* nothing and we *can do* nothing. It is His power within us that makes us able to fulfill our divine purpose in life. He receives glory and honor as we live *for* Him, and He lives *through* us.

In II Corinthians 12:9-10, Paul writes,

And He said to me, "My grace is sufficient for you, for My strength is made perfect in weakness. Therefore most gladly I will rather boast in my infirmities, that the power of Christ may rest upon me. Therefore I take pleasure in infirmities, in reproaches, in needs, in persecutions, in distresses, for Christ's sake. For when I am weak, then I am strong."

3

It has been said that life is ten percent what happens to us and ninety percent how we respond to it. Paul understood that his strength was not in himself, but that it was in the Lord Jesus, the One who pours His power into him. He is the strong One. Apostle Paul learned to trust the Lord with weak places. As a result, he fulfilled his divine purpose and took the Gospel of Jesus Christ to the Gentile nations, established churches, and also wrote three-fourths of the New Testament.

Scottish preacher James Stewart once said,

> It is always upon human weakness and humiliation, not human strength and confidence, that God chooses to build His kingdom; and that He can use us not merely in spite of our ordinariness and helplessness and disqualifying infirmities, but precisely because of them.

Our humiliations, struggles, battles, feelings of inadequacy, and weaknesses are truly what make us effective. They represent greatness because in our weaknesses we are right where God wants us, totally dependent upon Him and ready to embrace the power of Christ. It is in this place of total surrender that God will honor our honesty and admission of weakness and show Himself strong on our behalf.

Too many people are focused on themselves and their problems, or their pain and their lack. They are not focused on the divine call to walk in their purpose and do not realize He empowers us. A surrendered life is a fulfilled life. It is time to turn our eyes from all the

Apricot-Pecan Chicken Salad

MAKES 6 SERVINGS; **PREP:** 15 MIN.,
COOK: 5 MIN.

*Serve over salad greens with sliced avocado,
or grill between slices of whole grain bread
with Muenster cheese and fresh arugula.*

1 cup coarsely chopped pecans

3 cups chopped cooked chicken

1 cup chopped dried apricots

¼ cup mayonnaise

¼ cup sour cream

2 Tbsp. country-style Dijon mustard

2 Tbsp. honey

Salt and pepper to taste

1. Heat nuts in a small nonstick skillet over
medium-low heat, stirring often, 4 to 5
minutes or until toasted and fragrant.

2. Stir together chicken and next 5 ingredients in a large bowl. Season with salt
and pepper to taste; stir in pecans. Serve
immediately, or cover and chill until ready
to serve. Store in an airtight container in
refrigerator up to 3 days.

pain and grief that we have been through and make a choice to be loosed from the past and to walk into the purpose of our future.

The person who recognizes the divine pull on his life and follows that graced desire, yielding his life and future to the hand of the Potter, is in the majority. (Dr. Sam Sasser)

Joshua Follows His Destiny
Joshua 1:1-9

In the beginning of the book of Joshua, we see that Moses had died and Israel was in dire need of a leader who would hear from the Lord and then quickly obey Him. Joshua is told by the Lord in verse 2 to arise and go over the Jordan and take all of the people with him. In essence, the Lord was telling him that it was time for him to rise and walk into His purpose. God understood that Joshua had suffered loss and grief, but He still had a promised land for the people to possess. He still had a divine purpose to be fulfilled, and it was time for Joshua to take his place and lead the people into their inheritance.

Joshua didn't know all the trials and victories he would go through as he led the people, but he did not argue or make excuses. In verse 10, Joshua commanded the officers of the people to go through the camp and have the people prepare themselves for the journey. When he delivered the word of the Lord to them, Joshua walked obediently into his destiny as the next leader of God's people.

Did Joshua always know he would be the next leader? Did Moses tell him? Had God spoken to Him? Did he have fears? Did he wonder about his own ability to lead these people after what happened to Moses? Moses was the meekest man that ever walked the earth. There had never been a prophet like Moses, "whom the Lord knew face to face." With all of these virtues, Moses died before he entered the Promised Land because of one act of disobedience. Moses had been called, appointed, and anointed by Jehovah, but if he could not take God's people to the place promised to them, how could Joshua?

Could Joshua, Moses' assistant, truly lead these people? Joshua must have had some reservations. After all, he knew his own weak areas. I believe he answered the "call" because he had been in training for some time and deep in his soul, he knew this was his appointed time, his destiny. So by faith, Joshua stepped out onto that highway of obedience and faith. He had seen; he had heard; it was time. It was that day, the day when God would say "arise to your destiny."

Years of Training

Joshua's training began long before the events recorded in the book of Joshua. He had been born in Egypt, and except for Caleb, he was the only adult Israelite who survived the great exodus and 40 years of wandering in the wilderness, to enter the Promised Land.

In Numbers 14, Joshua and Caleb were two of the spies who went in to spy out Jericho. They returned with a victorious report of the land, while the other spies returned with a negative report. Joshua and Caleb were so grieved at the unbelief of the other spies' report that they tore their clothes, which was a sign of great grief and despair. They began to speak to the congregation of the children of Israel to believe that God was on their side. When the people refused to do so, God told them that only Joshua and Caleb would eventually enter the Promised Land. What a life lesson in the power of words spoken!

In Exodus 17:19 when Moses told Joshua to "choose men and go fight with Amalek." This brief statement shows us that Joshua already had the attention and trust of Moses. He had gained his confidence and was seen as a brave man who could be counted upon to go to war and lead others to fight and win! Moses explained to him that as Joshua fought down in the valley, he would be on top of the mountain with the rod of God in his hands. As long as Moses held up his hands, Joshua and Israel prevailed. Joshua defeated Amalek and his people with the edge of the sword. Joshua learned how to fight the battle and prevail at the instruction of Moses. The key to this victory was Joshua's obedience. He did not talk back nor object to Moses' instructions, but he immediately obeyed them and had great success against the enemy!

In Exodus 24:13, Joshua is called Moses' minister or assistant. The word "minister" in the Hebrew means to "serve, wait on, or be an attendant." Joshua was the servant of Moses. He followed him closely and learned what it meant to stay in the presence of God and have God talk to him face to face, as a friend. Joshua learned to serve with all of his heart, mind, and soul and make the vision of Moses' heart his own. Joshua learned what true submission was all about as he ministered to every need of the servant of God. He chose to stay by Moses' side during both the good and bad times.

The truth is, we cannot lead until we first learn to follow. We cannot walk in authority until we have learned obedience to authority.

Joshua was given the great honor of going halfway up the mountain with Moses when he received the Ten Commandments from God. He remained there waiting on the lower level as Moses drew near to the Lord. Joshua was left alone for 40 days and 40 nights (Exodus 24:18). What a test of his faith, patience and commitment!

Joshua was with Moses when God told him to go down the mountain for the people had corrupted themselves by making a golden calf to worship. (Exodus 32). Joshua heard the noise in the Israeli camp as he and Moses came down the mountain and thought it was the sound of war. Joshua "heard" the noise, but Moses "discerned" the noise. Moses was able to distinguish the power of sound from the sound of power. He could discern the fleshly display of sin from the spiritual manifestation of the presence of God. He knew that sound was not a sound that God would accept!

How many times in our singing or our praise is it merely form or religious activity? How many times are our prayers filled with religious clichés rather than heartfelt praise and worship? The Word says God is seeking those who worship Him in Spirit and in truth.

In Exodus 33:11, while Moses was in the tabernacle,

the Lord spoke to him face to face, as a man speaks to his friend. When Moses left the Tabernacle to go back to the camp, the Word says, "His servant Joshua, the son of Nun, a young man, did not depart from the Tabernacle." I believe Joshua was in awe of the presence of the Lord that he had just experienced and did not want to leave this place for the glory of the Lord surrounded him. Who knows what God might have said to him as he lingered in His presence?

How quickly we tend to leave the presence of the Lord. I wonder what He would say to us if we would just stay a while with Him? We need to learn to wait in silence and hear the Lord as He speaks.

There is an account in Numbers 11:16-30 in which God speaks to Moses to get 70 elders to stand together with him in the Tabernacle of Meeting. "The Lord came down in a cloud and spoke unto him and took of the Spirit that was upon him and put the same Spirit upon the 70 elders so that they could help Moses bear the burden of the people." There were two elders that for some reason had remained in the camp and were prophesying. A young man thought this was strange, so he ran to tell Moses. In verse 28, Joshua asked Moses to forbid those men to prophesy. This act shows Joshua's character. He himself did not go and rebuke the elders and neither did he ask Moses to kill them. It was the love and faithfulness to his master that caused him to say anything. Moses' reply was, "Enviest thou for my sake"? But there was no jealousy or self-seeking promotion here on Joshua's part. His only concern was for the honor of Moses, the one he served! This was a display of Moses'

humility and no doubt a lesson to Joshua, that true
leaders are not threatened by God's display of His gifts
or His presence in others.

Many people I see today probably would not have
learned that lesson so quickly or quietly. They would
have wanted to voice their opinion. How we need teach-
able spirits! How much quicker we would begin to fulfill
our purpose if we truly would walk as submitted, worshipping servants. We must grasp the truth that disobedience will only cause delays or unplanned detours
along the road of destiny.

Joshua's Leadership Role

In Numbers 27, the Lord told Moses to lay hands on
Joshua and commission him in the sight of the priest
and all of Israel. This was a confirming sign to Israel of
Joshua's future leadership role.

Moses spoke to all of Israel in Deuteronomy 31 and
told them that he could no longer discharge his duties
because of his advancing age and God's command that
he should not cross over the Jordan. He told them that
Joshua would lead them into their inheritance.

Joshua was full of the Spirit and full of wisdom because Moses had laid hands on him. Deuteronomy 34:9
says that because Moses laid hands on him in the eyes of
the people, they heeded him and did as the Lord had
commanded Moses. The action of Moses shows us the
importance of visibility of the actions of leaders.

Joshua went through a long process of growth and
maturity to be the leader that God had purposed him to
be. He did not jump into a place of leadership when he

desired it, but it was all in God's time and season. In the first chapter of Joshua, verses 1 and 2, God told him "My servant Moses is dead. It is now time for you to arise and go over this Jordan, you and all the people, to the land which I am giving them."

It was now time for Joshua to arise and walk in his purpose. We can see from the above passages that Joshua had experienced many life lessons and had been taught and trained to understand the heart of a godly leader. What we need to understand is that everything that we experience in our lives, the good and the bad, is all part of the learning process that leads us on the road of divine destiny.

You may say, "I have made too much of a mess of my life. Who am I? What can I do for the Lord?" In Jeremiah 18:1-6, we see the answer to the dilemma of wrong choices. Jeremiah cried, "God is the Potter!" God was willing to clean up the mess Israel had made. And today He is willing to remake us into another vessel that will please Him. Our day is not over if we will just yield the marred clay of our earthly existence into the Master Potter's hands. It is there that He will remake us.

As I write this I can hear some of you say, "Oh come on. That was Joshua. He was walking with Moses. He had never been in sin, and he really didn't make any wrong choices. He didn't mess his life up. I have made too many wrong choices. God can't use me. There is no way I have a divine purpose. How can God use me?"

God has a plan and He is powerful enough to bring it about no matter what our mistakes have been.

CHAPTER TWO

LEAST LIKELIES

You are exactly who God wants! He specializes in the "least likelies." I remember one night some years ago, I was in the prayer room with the choir, which I directed at that time. We were spending time in prayer before the service began. I looked around the room and saw grown men standing crying, lifting their hands in the presence of the Lord; and the ladies, unaware of anyone else, were lost in the glory of the Lord's presence. As I looked at each of these people, I began to weep. Having worked with them so long, I knew most of their pasts. There were ex-drug addicts, alcoholics, those who I knew had been abused, and even a couple of ladies who were in abusive marriages. Some of them had been raised with not very much of this world's goods. Not many of them really had a loving, blessed past to look back upon, but there they stood, enveloped in our Savior's love.

At that moment, God spoke to me. "I know you wonder: 'Lord, how can you anoint us? We don't really have a lot to offer You?' But I don't see as you see. I choose to anoint the least likelies, the ones nobody else thinks can amount to anything. I grow them up and use them for My glory."

I began to cry like a baby. "Oh thank You, Lord. I know I am a least likely so thank You for Your grace that touches my life."

I thought back on my life. Before I understood the truth of God's desire to use our lives and that we all have a divine destiny, I was filled with all kinds of intimidation. I even questioned my very existence from time to time. I was always comparing myself with everybody else. Most of the time I felt I would never measure up.

I was born into a Christian family, which I thank God for. My dad was a pastor and a preacher of preachers. He had the heart of a true shepherd and loved his people. To be honest, I have not heard many who had such revelation as he had been given.

My mother was and still is, an anointed woman of God, an intercessor, a helpmeet and a servant of servants. You have probably met her—the Proverbs 31 woman.

My brother, at 17, directed our 120 voice youth choir. He was gifted musically and vocally, and more than that, the anointing saturated his very being. At nineteen years of age, he signed a contract with Word Music in Nashville to write and record music. My younger brother, at 13, played the trumpet in school and in the church band. He was very good looking and even made straight As in school. I was literally surrounded by talent and ability.

I would look at everyone around me and then I would look at me, the pastor's daughter. I always felt like some loved me because of who I was and some hated me because of that. I wasn't as gifted in music as my brother. I didn't make straight As. I was just me, searching for my place.

Did I have a purpose? What was I created for? Where was my life going? The enemy had me right where he wanted me. I pushed and pulled my way throughout my childhood and teen years, trying to find my place. I was focused in the wrong place. Along the way, I made wrong decisions and some wrong choices, but thank God for praying parents who cried out for me. Finally, one day I chose to take the right road! Somehow, just in making this choice, I began to feel free. I began to turn my focus on what I *could be* rather than what I wasn't, or thought I *could never be*. I turned my focus toward my heavenly Father.

We focus on the seen instead of the unseen. We focus on what we have or what we are, what we look like or what we can or cannot do, while all the time, none of this is what God wants from us. Eve did the same thing when she disobeyed. She had a whole garden of trees, fruits, and vegetables, more than she could ever delight in. But the enemy caused her to focus on the ONE tree, the ONE apple she was not supposed to have. She was deceived and chose to obey the wrong voice! She never reached her full potential because her focus was wrong.

Where are you focused? Get your eyes off yourself and what you don't have, can't have, or don't look like and begin to look to our Lord. He declares the end from the beginning. It doesn't matter where you have been or what you have done, turn to Him. It doesn't matter how many wrong choices you have made, He will remake you. Get up into the hands of the Potter as Jeremiah cried out and let Him have all of you.

14

A Harlot's Destiny

The story of Rahab is found in the second chapter of Joshua. Joshua sent two men to spy out the surrounding area, especially Jericho. Joshua wanted to know about the place he was going to lead the people into and possibly go to war with. That was not a lack of faith, it was wisdom and the mark of a great leader.

The two spies came to the house of a harlot named Rahab. They stayed there to rest before finishing the journey ahead of them. The king of Jericho was told about the men and sent word to Rahab to bring the men to him. She did not obey his command. Instead she hid the men and helped them to escape. In providing these men with safety and a means of escape, she sealed her own destiny and did not have to face the wrath of the king of the destruction of Jericho.

In verse 15 of chapter 2, we are told that she let the men down by a rope through a window. Her house was part of the city wall. Rahab was not a Jew, but rather she was a Gentile. She was of the Amorites, a race that was committed to the destruction of the Jewish nation. She had been involved in the vilest of sins, selling her body to make a living. She was a "least likely" in every way.

The City of Jericho did not observe the Sabbath. There was no Bible to read and no prophets to send the message. Yet amazingly in verse nine, Rahab said to the two men of Israel, "I know the Lord has given you the land and your terror has fallen upon us and all of the people who live in the land are fainthearted because of you." They had already heard how the Lord dried up the water of the Red Sea for them when they came out of

Egypt and how Israel utterly destroyed the two kings of the Amorites on the east side of the Jordan.

In verse 11, Rahab, the harlot, who did not know God and was taught to hate all Jews, told the men that when they heard the word of all of Israel's victories, their hearts melted and that no man or woman had spirit or courage. She said about the God of Israel, "The Lord your God, He is God in heaven above and on earth beneath."

Now to understand the greatness of this statement, imagine if one of Osama Bin Ladin or Saddam Hussein's men begin to confess Jesus Christ as Lord of all! There is no history recorded in Rahab's life of her ever knowing about God or being taught about Him. It is just the opposite. Being from the Amorite people, she would have been taught to hate the God of Israel and His people. She showed great courage and faith to ask for the men to save her and her family. God, in His sovereign plan and purpose, chose Rahab to help carry the righteous bloodline. It was the scarlet cord, which represented the blood of Christ that identified her house and brought great salvation.

God knew she was a woman of divine destiny. Believing, repentance and obedience work hand in hand. The safety of Rahab and her household was contingent upon her obedience to the instructions of God's messengers. Her instructions were as follows:

1. She was not to mention their business or betray them to their enemies and she must be loyal to them and promote their interests. This would be a sign of love for the brethren.

2. She must place the scarlet cord in the window so that her house might be recognized. This scarlet cord would identify her home and separate it from others. In the same way we must bear the identity mark of God's children. The blood of Jesus cleanses us from our sins and makes us one.

3. She must abide in her house until they came for her. We too must keep separate from the world.

In verse 21 she said, "According to your word, so be it." There was no resentment, no objections, just obedience, and she bound the scarlet line in the window. She displayed her redemption by her obedience. The reward of her faith and obedience was that "she perished not with them that believed not." Her choice to obey was an indication of her belief. Rahab's choice to walk in her destiny saved not only her own life, but the life of all those in her family.

When we choose to walk in our destiny and our purpose, the lives of others around us will also be affected. Whether we walk in our purpose or we choose not to, everyone around us in the present and the future will be touched by what we do.

In Joshua 6:25 it says of Rahab, "She dwells in Israel to this day." Rahab went from being a citizen of a heathen nation to being given a place in the congregation of Israel, God's chosen people. Second Chronicles 2:11 tell us that she married Salmon, who was a prince of Judah. The Tribe of Judah was the most praised, the greatest in number, and the most dignified. Think about it, a harlot, saved through her obedience, who had no dignity and lived a life of shameful disgrace, was now a part of the most dignified tribe of Israel.

The Tribe of Judah camped closest to the Tabernacle, which is a type of being closest to the Lord Himself! Only the grace of God can move us from shame to dignity. Rahab's purpose does not stop with the scarlet cord. In reading the genealogy of Jesus Christ in the book of Matthew, the list reads: Nashon, Salmon, Boaz, Obed, Jesse, David, Jesus Christ. Rahab became the honored wife of a prince in Judah, the mother of Boaz, and one of King David's grandmothers. She was one of the favored ancestors of the Lord Jesus Christ our Savior. Obedience can move us into a glorious position that we did not know existed.

Rahab was delivered from sin and shame and rose to soaring heights of honor and dignity. Don't let the enemy keep you in the pit of darkness and despair. Arise and walk in the life of His Word and walk into your divine purpose!

Whether like Joshua, trained from birth by his mentor to fulfill his destiny, or like Rahab, born into a life without God or any teacher, with no hope and in the darkness of sin, God still has a divine destiny for you to fulfill. It doesn't matter when you start. It is never too late.

God wants vessels of endurance. He wants vessels who can take the heat of the furnace. He wants those who will not stop short, who won't quit no matter how rocky the road or how high the hill. The word "endurance" means "to have fortitude, remain, bear trials, persevere, abide."

Our heavenly Father wants men and women who are willing to be filled daily with His presence and His purpose. He seeks people who are willing to sit at His feet and who are ready to be poured out in worship and in service! The Greek root word for "tarry" means "to take your seat here and learn your lesson." How we need to tarry in the presence of our Father.

Second Timothy 2:1-12 shows us that endurance is the key to victory. It is not the one who runs the fastest, but it is the one who runs to the end.

Each of us has divine purpose. God has chosen us. He has written a book about our lives. All of our lives, every day of our lives, our Father is pulling us toward that purpose. We have to make a choice to walk in our divine purpose or choose to go our own way. We will, without a doubt, face a critical time of decision whether to walk into or run away from that which God has prepared for us, no matter what the cost.

When you face that time and that decision, which road will you choose? Will you choose the road of divine destiny or the road of self will, which only leads to destruction? It's time to choose!

CHAPTER THREE

OBEDIENCE ENSURES PROTECTION

A few months ago God spoke this word to my heart: "Many of my people are imprisoned in hurts and failures of the past. They have allowed the offense to take root in the depths of their soul, and they have bound themselves into an unproductive web of thoughts and emotions. They are paralyzed from within and bitterness has taken comfort in the surroundings of a wounded spirit. They are no longer living, only existing. They live in a motionless past, with no direction for today and no dreams for the future. The key to a fulfilled life is evidenced in their obedience to My Word. Tell them I love them. There is hope in Me. Teach them truth, the truth of My Word! They can know Me through My Word! They can be healed, and they can be whole!"

All my life I have been surrounded by men and women of God: my parents, grandfather, great-grandfather, cousins, and then I married into a pastor's home and both of my husband's parents were preachers. As a result, I am aware of the many problems that people face in life. Almost daily someone would call or come to our home searching for direction in their life, deliverance, or maybe just a simple hug. I have witnessed, first-hand, the devastation in people's lives. I have also been blessed to see many who have come to Christ very broken, willing, and submissive to do whatever it took to get their lives on track. God's grace produced loving restoration In these people.

When they made the choice to come to the Lord and ask Him into their hearts, they immediately began to grow and become faithful members of the family of God. As they grew and matured in Christ, little by little their lives got on track and healing brought wholeness, and wholeness brought restoration.

On the other hand, there are some who come to the altar, attempt to live for Christ, and then in no time, they fall back into the same pattern of sin and defeat. I have often wondered what the difference was. Why do some go on and pursue their destiny, and others only make a false start? In Joshua 1:3-9, we will see some principles that will give us the answers.

The first principle in learning how to grow in God and walk in our purpose is to have a "made-up mind" when we come to the Lord. We need to come to Him, repentant and broken. It requires more than shedding a tear or having an emotion. We need to have the desperation of knowing we cannot go any further, and so we desire to live for Him.

The second principle is that we must develop a deep hunger for the Word. Consistent studying, meditating, and speaking the Word is an important part of our maturity in God. Knowing the Word means that we continually think about it so that it will become the compass of our lives and direct the way we live.

21

Some people never go any deeper in God than what their emotions will allow. They live strictly by their feelings. If they *feel* like reading the Word, they will. If they *feel* like praying, they will. If they *feel* like going to church, they will. It is all about how they *feel*. Although there is nothing wrong with feelings and emotions God created us to have, but they are not to rule or control us. Emotions are fickle. They change day by day, hour by hour, minute by minute. They are neither right nor wrong, they just are. We have to allow the Word to take root in our spirit so that we can rule our emotions. If our emotions rule, we will say the wrong thing and act the wrong way. When our emotions subside, we wish we could take everything back. I know. I have been there.

The battle always begins in our mind. We are what we think about. Proverbs 23:7 says, "As a man thinketh in his heart, so is he." If you allow a thought to stay in your mind, it will go from your mind to your heart and when it reaches your heart, it has potential to control you and it is here, in this place, you become what you think.

Personal Testimony

During my junior high years, I struggled overwhelmingly with unforgiveness and so I was living in direct disobedience to God's Word. In Matthew 18, the disciples asked Jesus how many times they should forgive an individual who wronged them. He told them seventy times seven, which is 490 times per day. It literally means that we should walk with the attitude of forgiveness in our hearts at all times. Because I didn't, that one stronghold opened the door for the enemy to gain control of my mind.

As stated earlier, my dad was a pastor for as long as I can remember. During the 1970s, our church averaged 900-950 in attendance. There was one man in the congregation who just could not stand my dad. (Later I found out he had been raised in an orphanage and had never learned to submit to any authority.) My dad was a very loving shepherd, and he was also a man of integrity and godly order. My dad was the pastor of the church, and loving people was his life. He was aware that this man did not like him, and Dad didn't like it when people didn't like him. As a result, he would go out of his way to speak to this person to try and bring peace between them, unfortunately without any success.

I remember an elderly lady passing away in our church. As always, Dad went to the funeral home to be with the family. I remember standing by my dad when this particular man walked up to the casket. My dad put his arm around him, and he jerked away and told dad to leave him alone. I looked into my dad's eyes. Pain brought him to the brink of tears. He looked so hurt. Once again, he had reached out only to be rejected. That made me so mad! How could he do that to my dad; right here, right now? Things like that happened many times, although the majority of the people loved us and were good to us.

I allowed offenses that did occur to cause me to resent people. I did not understand it because my dad and mom were loving, praying people who were giving their lives for the people they pastored. At 13 years of age, I wanted that man to suffer. That feeling stayed in my heart a long time. I didn't realize that by allowing that unforgiveness and bitterness, I was holding myself in bondage. The enemy was gaining access in my life through that open door.

My mind would constantly be filled with thoughts of hatred and wanting to see those hurt who hurt my family. My mind was becoming a web of destructive thoughts, and I was too young to know I really needed help. I would sit in church and remove myself through my thoughts to another place and another time. I can remember several times my dad had to get my attention by snapping his fingers to bring me back to reality. My dad and mom were worried about me. They did not know what was wrong. I didn't know what was wrong either, so I couldn't tell them. As always, they began to pray for me.

For one year, my heart was so hard that I could not cry. I learned to play a game. On the outside, I acted as if everything were fine. On the inside, where no one could see, I felt alone and hopeless. If you give the enemy an opening into your life, he will rush in with one purpose—to forever separate you from God. I have come to understand it was not so much that the devil wanted me, but in destroying me, he hurt the heart of God. He uses us to get to God!

In the midst of this, my dad picked me up after school one day to my surprise. He said he had come to take me out to eat, just him and me. I liked that, but I didn't realize at the time that his ulterior motive was to get me to talk. He looked straight into my eyes and asked, "Sissy, what can I do to help you? What is wrong?" I told him I really couldn't explain it because I didn't understand what was happening to me. With tears in his eyes, he told me how much he and Mom loved me and that they would always be there for me. I knew that. One thing I always knew—my parents loved me. That's what made it all so hard. I hadn't wanted to hurt them, but I was doing so by my behavior. As I blankly stared out the window, we drove home in silence, neither of us knowing what to say.

I had confided in a friend that the only reason I was continuing to go to church was out of respect for my parents. Not many days after that, Mom and Dad confronted me. My friend had contacted my parents about what I had shared with her. I realize now, she told them because she was concerned about me, but at fourteen years of age, it looked and felt like betrayal. I allowed it to drive the bitterness deeper.

One Saturday night, I was upstairs in my room getting ready to go to church when I heard a knock at my door. It was my parents. For a moment, they just looked at me, and then said, "Diane, if you don't want to go to church, you don't have to go. We appreciate that you respect us, but we want you to go to church because you love the Lord, and you want to be in His presence."

They had adhered to principle. This was an illustration of their trust in God and their genuine confidence that His Word would work. They knew that they had been obedient and faithful in training me and my brothers, and now they decided to trust me to choose to walk in the truth I had been taught.

To be honest, their reaction both frightened and sad-
dened me. My childish thought was surely they wouldn't
leave me alone and just go without me. I knew I had hurt
them. I didn't mean to, but I had! The look in their eyes
was more than I could take. They turned and walked out
of my room. I sat speechless and wide-eyed on the edge
of my bed, filled with so many thoughts and emotions.
Suddenly I jumped up and finished getting ready. I had to
go that night. I didn't want mom and dad to hurt anymore, and I didn't want to hurt God's heart either.

When God has His hands on our lives, He never
stops drawing us. He protects us even when we don't
know He is doing it. Because He loves us and has a des-
tined plan for our lives, His grace leads and protects us
before we even know we need His direction or His protection. His grace goes ahead of us to prevent anything
from happening to us that God does not agree with.

I will never forget one Saturday afternoon. The
friend I had confided in called and asked me to come to
her house. When I arrived, she asked me to have a seat.
She had been in prayer for me just that morning and
God had spoken to her spirit and tell her that it was now
time for her to talk to me and clear up any misunder-
standings between us. "God wants to touch you today,"
she told me. "I would never hurt you and when you confided in me concerning going to church, I became very
troubled. I felt inadequate by myself to help you."

I felt myself beginning to tense up and get defensive.
As she continued, she began to cry and tell me that she
loved me and God loved me and He had a plan and a
purpose for my life. She said that it was time for me to

let go of the past and all of its pain and move forward into God's plan.

I tried to stop the emotions, but the dam broke and my insides began to tremble. I started crying for the first time in a year. We prayed together, cried together, and I hugged her and told her I loved her. God had begun the healing process in me and it all started with the words "forgive me."

Is there someone you have hurt? Maybe you didn't mean to, or maybe they hurt you. It is time to let go of everything. Talk to them. Tell them you love them. Make peace. God will help you. The release that comes makes everything worth it. Someone has to be the bigger person and bring peace!

Matthew 5:9 says, "Blessed are the peacemakers, For they shall be called the sons of God." This scripture calls us sons, not babies. It speaks of maturity in Christ. When we make peace and walk in an attitude of forgiveness, God looks at us as mature sons and daughters. He sees us as friends with whom He delights in sharing His dreams.

I went home and when my mom saw me, she knew something had happened. I told her what had just taken place. She screamed for my dad. He came running and for the first time, in a long while, I embraced both of my parents as we cried and praised the Lord together. I felt such freedom. I ran up to my room and began to pray. I asked the Lord to forgive me and to show me His ways. I truly committed myself to Him that day. Principle had protected me and for that, I am so thankful!

When you are bound, you don't realize you are

holding others in bondage also. You are shutting them out. I have learned that the walls I put up to protect myself from people were the very walls that kept the people out who could have ministered to me. We will never make a choice that will affect or hurt only us. Everything about us affects everyone around us! Allowing unforgiveness to settle into my heart was in direct disobedience to God's Word. I was violating principle and for a long time, I suffered the consequence of a hard heart.

Matthew 6:12, "And forgive us our debts, AS we forgive our debtors." This scripture leaps off of the page to me; specifically the "as." This verse is part of the prayer that Jesus taught the disciples how to pray. This verse says we will only be forgiven for our transgressions to the degree that we have forgiven others who have hurt or transgressed us. If we want forgiveness, we must forgive. We reap what we sow (Galatians 6:7). If we do not forgive, we will not be forgiven. It is really that simple! I have a made up mind, and by His grace, I choose to walk in forgiveness!

CHAPTER FOUR

TAKING ACTION

We must learn to guard our minds and emotions. We have to be diligent in studying the Word and be committed to a specific time of prayer. Discipline produces desire, and a desire fulfilled produces delight! As you discipline yourself to read the Word and to pray, the desire inside of you to know the Father more intimately will increase. The deeper you know Him, the greater the delight He brings to your heart and soul! Your cry will be "More Father, more of You!"

Song of Solomon 1:2 says, "Draw us away, we will run after You." It is the Father who draws us and gives us the desire to know Him. It is the Holy Spirit that pours out His love into our hearts that causes us to love Him.

"O Lord, we want to know You in a deeper way than ever before. Please draw us by Your spirit and teach us Your way and Your will."

The Word tells us in Philippians 4:8 to only think about or meditate on things that are true, noble, just, pure, lovely, or of a good report. What do you think about? What has your mind been dwelling on today? That is where the problem starts. We need to demand that our mind think on good things. It can help to put on praise music. We should not look back to the problems of the past, but look ahead to Jesus, the beginning and the ending of our faith.

In Romans 12:2, we are told to renew (refresh, restore, replenish, restock) our minds, that is to fill our minds over and over again with pure thoughts by the Word of the Lord, so that we will not be conformed to the world. The Word that we know will keep us in the time of trouble and will many times keep us out of trouble.

Obedience Is Hearing and Doing

In verses Joshua 3-5, we read of the promises that God gave Joshua. It explains that God had given him every place the "sole of his foot" would walk upon. The Lord further explained the boundaries of the territory given to Joshua and the children of Israel and then He reassured Joshua that He would always be with him and never forsake him, and that no man would be able to stand before him for as long as he lived. What divine assurances! What divine protection! What a way to start on a journey! God promised His continued presence with Joshua, and His presence secures success.

I have found that with every promised blessing, there is a prerequisite of obedience. The key to any blessing in life is that we walk in obedience to every word that God says. In verse 7, the Lord told Joshua to be strong and courageous and obey all of the law, not turning to the right or to the left. The Lord even promised him prosperity as a reward to obedience.

Taking Action

In verse 8, Joshua was told to never let the Word leave his mouth: "speak My Word, keep it ever before you and meditate in the Word, both day and night!" The reason many people are depressed, bitter, unforgiving, angry, and have no hope is because they do not fill their mind and heart with the Word of the Lord. It is not enough just to hear a sermon preached on Sunday, we must take time every day to read the Word and listen to it with our spirit!

Joshua was told by God to "meditate" on the Word. The word "meditate," in Hebrew, indicates a continual recounting of His words. That is why it says that the Book of the Law (v8), will not depart from our mouth. The Word must become life to you. There must be a speaking, hearing and then doing.

> Do not merely listen to the Word and so deceive yourselves. Do what it says. Anyone who listens to the Word but does not do what it says is like a man who looks at his face in a mirror and, after looking at himself, goes away and immediately forgets what he looks like. But the man who looks intently into the perfect law that gives freedom, and continues to do this, not forgetting what he has heard, but doing it—he will be blessed in what he does (James 1:22-25).

The one who only hears the Word will soon forget it, but the one who hears it and acts out the Word is the one that will have a blessed life. God gave Israel the "promised land," but if they were going to possess it, they had to live their lives in obedience to the Divine Law of Jehovah!

The Lord Jesus Christ died for every man, woman, boy and girl. All of us can come to Him and be born again. After we are born again, we are not free to just live as we please. We have been given the Word of God to read and understand and to obey. And when we obey, we are blessed!

So, since Christ suffered in the flesh, for us, for you, arm yourselves with the same thought and purpose (patiently to suffer rather than fail to please God). For whoever has suffered in the flesh, (having the mind of Christ) is done with (intentional) sin, (has stopped pleasing himself and the world and pleases God.) So that he can no longer spend the rest of his natural life living by (his) human appetites and desires, but (he lives) for what God wills (I Peter 4:1-2 AMP)

Knowledge of the Word by itself will not cause us to grow spiritually. The Pharisees, some of the religious leaders of Jesus' day, were required to be able to quote the first five books of the Old Testament. Head knowledge and heart knowledge, however, are two different things. As we walk in obedience to what we know, we will grow and mature in God. The more we see Him, the more we desire Him. The deeper we know Him, the greater our obedience to Him. Our reason for not sinning is not just because we are afraid of the consequences if we get caught, but by the grace of God, we stop sinning because we don't want to hurt the heart of God. Genuine revelation refines the motives for our actions. The man or woman, who is self-ruled, opposes the Word and the will of God!

"Therefore, submit to God, resist the devil and he will flee from you" (James 4:7). The Hebrew word for "submit" means "our reflex to obey." The 1828 *Webster's Dictionary* says that the word "submit" means "to resign or surrender to the power, will or authority of another." It means to "yield without murmuring!"

We can do something we are told to do, but if we murmur and complain, we are not submitted! There is a story I heard my dad tell one time that illustrates this principle. There was a little boy in school and he was always talking and disrupting the class. The teacher said to him one day, "Tommy, go to the corner and stand until I tell you that you can be seated." He reluctantly went to the corner. While standing there he murmured, "I may be standing up on the outside, but inside I am sitting down!" It is this attitude that will cause us to struggle all through our lives, rather than to enjoy the promised blessings of God.

The Hebrew word for "resist" means literally, "to stand against." It is a picture of a mound or a dam that stands strong as the current or water comes rushing by. The dam is unmoved and unharmed as it passively stands in its place. Again to my trusty 1828 Webster's, "resist" means "a fixed body which interrupts the passage of a moving body, as in the action of force to stop, repel or defeat progress."

Ephesians 6:13-14 says, "Therefore take up the

whole armor of God, that you may be able to withstand in the evil day, and having done all, to stand...Stand therefore..." These two scriptures tell us to stand. When we've done all that we can to prepare ourselves, we need to stand in the strength and the rest of the Lord.

I am aware of the principle of "spiritual warfare." There are many times God will direct me to pray against a particular stronghold until it is brought down. However, I believe if we will submit every area of our lives to God, no matter what it costs us, and walk in obedience, we are building up a resistance to the enemy in our lives. The enemy will try to come at us, but when he sees we will not be moved from our "stand" or our obedience to the Father, he will run in terror. Living our lives submitted to God in humble obedience causes the enemy to run!

Jesus told us that we were the light of the world. Submission produces obedience and obedience will bring the light of His glorious presence into our lives. That light shining through us, dispels the darkness!

The key to the success of Joshua as the leader of Israel was that early on, he learned to obey the Word of the Lord. He kept the Word before him continually. The Lord told him as long as he kept God's Word before him, and walked in it, his way would be blessed and prosperous.

Could it be that the areas of disobedience in our lives have stopped the blessings of the Lord? If obedience worked for Joshua, it will work for us today because our Father says it will!

Examine your heart. Are things going right for you?

Are your prayers being answered? Take off the mask and be real. If there are things contrary to the Word of the Lord, repent and begin to walk on that road of submission and obedience.

There is a principle of spiritual warfare that we can pull down strongholds, using the mighty weapons of God. There are times God will show us a specific spirit that has to be brought down through prayer and the truth of the Word, but if we will submit every area of our lives, no matter what it costs us, walking in obedience builds up the resistance in our lives. The enemy may try to come at us, but when he sees that we will not be moved and we will not hurt the heart of God by disobedience, the Word says he will flee from us, which in the Greek means "to run in terror."

We have to build up our resistance to the enemy by walking in obedience and submission to every word of the Lord. If we are submitted to the Lord, we will shine with the light of His presence, and that light will dispel any darkness!

CHAPTER FIVE

TAKING PERSONAL RESPONSIBILITY

Can a mother forget the baby at her breast and have no compassion on the child she has borne? Though she may forget, I will not forget you! See, I have engraved you on the palm of My hands; your walls are ever before me (Isaiah 49:15-16).

Evangelist Leighton Ford once said, "God loves us the way we are, but He loves us too much to leave us that way!"

When Jesus walked the earth over 2000 years ago, He saw a great tragedy. It says in Matthew 9:36-38 that He saw the multitudes of people and He was moved with great compassion for them. They were like sheep without a shepherd. They had no direction and were wandering aimlessly without any vision or goals. They were not being taught the Word or the way of the Lord, so they didn't know to live and how to fulfill the purpose for which they had been created. He told the disciples to pray that laborers would go forth to gather the harvest. He knew that the people needed to be loved and cared for, to be taught, and to be trained in the truth of His Word.

I see the same scenario today—people who are wandering aimlessly, without any direction or vision in their lives. They have no idea of the plans and purposes of God for them and for His church. My heart cries out, "O Lord, send forth laborers, men and women of God, who are filled with Your love, Your character, Your holiness, Your vision, Your truth, anointed to go forth in Your name and be all that You meant for Your church to be and do all that You meant for us to do." My heart's desire is to see people begin to grow in the Lord and understand who they are in God and what He has prepared for them, right here and now.

Then Joshua commanded the officers of the people saying, "Pass through the camp and command the people, saying, 'Prepare provisions for yourselves, for within three days you will cross over this Jordan, to go in to possess the land which the Lord your God is giving you to possess (Joshua 1:10-11).

...and they commanded the people, saying, "When you see the ark of the covenant of the Lord your God, and the priests, the Levites, bearing it, then you shall set out from your place and go after it. Yet there shall be a space between you and it, about two thousand cubits by measure. Do not come near it, that you may know the way by which you must go, for, you

have not passed this way before. And Joshua said to the people, "Sanctify yourselves, for tomorrow the Lord will do wonders among you (Joshua 3:3-5).

The command was for each person in the Israeli camp to prepare by taking personal responsibility to make themselves ready to walk into their divine inheritance. This was a command from Joshua. He did not say, "If you want to, or if you feel like it," which is the way many people want to live their lives. The children of Israel were instructed to prepare their own provisions. Joshua was saying to them, "We are now entering into a new dimension. You have not passed this way before." The welfare system and the streets are full of people who have either never heard or never heeded the truth. Sadly, the church is filled with many as well. It is now time for each one of us to learn what it means to stand in the secret place, hidden in the arms of our Lord. We must believe and understand that no matter what takes place around us, He will keep us safe!

God was now developing, in His people, a mentality of personal responsibility. It was time for each of them to follow the Word of the Lord. Up until this time, God had provided everything for them. They had survived totally by the power and the supernatural provision of God Himself.

They had seen the ten plagues sent by God come upon the Egyptians and their leader, Pharaoh, which resulted in the people of God being released from more than 400 years of bondage. During the last 40 years of journeying in the desert, they had seen God rain down manna to feed them. When bread wasn't enough, He rained down quail. All they had to do was gather the food from the ground.

But even in gathering the food, He had a pattern that they should follow. Obedience to His divine pattern was the key to their being filled. When they were cold, He sent them a fire by night to warm and lead them and then a cloud by day to show them the way. All they had to do was keep their eyes focused. They had seen the mountains shake with His glory and heard His thunderous voice as He spoke.

His presence and power had led them by their natural sight, but a new day was dawning. Moses was dead. All of those who had come out of Egypt (except for Joshua and Caleb) had died in the wilderness because of unbelief. There was now a new generation being led by a new leader. It was a new day of circumcision, a new day of faith and trust! They would now hear from God by faith, not by natural sight!

Before God had taken care of them like children. In the past he had called Moses into His presence and spoken to him concerning His people. Then Moses was instructed to tell the people what God had said. Now it was time for each one to take personal responsibility to hear and to obey. There would be new directions given and each one was responsible to follow the new commands. It would be up to each individual to obey, in order to possess their possessions!

Oh how this word is ringing in my ears and piercing through my heart! Each one of us today must hear and understand that no one can accept Jesus for us, read the Word for us, walk in the Spirit for us, or fulfill our divine purpose. We have to take personal responsibility for who and what we are.

Testimony

I have two sons, fifteen and seventeen. Both of them have Jesus in their hearts and except for a few teenage quirks, there have never been any real problems with them. My oldest son is very athletic and loves to play basketball and baseball. From the first year of tee ball until his junior year, he had always been picked to be on the All-Star teams to play second base and lead off in the batting order, or be a part of the starting five. The only drawback that he has ever had is that he is not as tall as most of the other players.

When you are a small child, your speed and your talent will get you through. As he began to get older, the other boys were quickly passing him by when it came to height and weight. His coach told him he had quick hands, a great shot, and was a good ball handler., but the same coach eventually cut him from the team because he wasn't tall enough. His first impulse was to never try out for basketball again.

One day Cody came to us and said, "I am going to begin an exercise program of lifting weights. I cannot help it that I am not as tall as the other guys, but I can become just as strong, even stronger. Next year when I try out, that coach will regret the day he ever cut me from the team!" Wow! My son was going to take a negative situation and turn it into a positive one. To myself I thought, *I am proud of your attitude, Cody, but son, this is going to take a lot of discipline on your part. Do you have the 'stick-to-it' discipline that you need, or is this just an emotion because of what you are going through?*

I watched my son for months, discipline himself every night. Without fail, he worked out with a friend for two hours. He drank horrible tasting protein drinks twice a day, and no matter what he may have to miss doing with his other friends, he keeps up the discipline. I asked him one day, "Cody, why are you doing all of this?" He said to me, "Mom, I am not tall. I have to work harder to gain a place on the team. I know what the outcome of all of this will be. I will be stronger and in better shape. I won't have to feel that 'less than' feeling anymore. I can't do anything about how tall I am, but I can do something about how strong I am." And now that we are all seeing the results of this disciplined routine, he has a greater desire than ever to be in shape.

It's great how God will take the natural situations of life and teach us a spiritual truth. In Cody's case, he knew he had to do something to make himself physically better. He chose to be disciplined and get in shape. As a result of the discipline, he is getting himself into better shape than any of his friends. The discipline came from a desire to be better. The benefits of the discipline create a desire to be more disciplined.

It is the same way with us and the Lord in our relationship to Him. If we look around at others, many of them may seem to be passing us by in their spiritual growth. As a result of their growth, they seem to have joy and peace. They may have problems, but they go through them with a smile and a praise. The pastor even approaches them to teach a class and the choir director wants them to sing in the choir.

41

If we think, "Here I am, with no joy or purpose, and no one asks me to do anything," we need to ask ourselves if we have taken personal responsibility for our situation or do we depend on everyone else to pray for us, teach us, or hear from the Lord. Are you disciplined in any area of your life? Like Cody, we need to stop looking at what we don't have and make something better of what we do have.

Laziness

One of the greatest hindrances of discipline is just plain laziness. We want to feel like reading the Word, or praying or going to church or witnessing. Our flesh will hardly ever want to do any of these things. That is what discipline means. It means we do what you need to do, not because we feel like it, but because we know the outcome of it will get us to the place you need to be in the realm of the Spirit. To know God, we must spend time with Him in prayer, taking time to listen to Him. Prayer is a two-way conversation, we need to give Him time to speak back. We also need to read and study His Word and fellowship and become a part of His body, the Church. We must be faithful and diligent, not making a good start and then giving up because we don't feel like it anymore. We need to discipline ourselves to be with the Lord, whether we're tired or not because He rewards faithfulness.

One characteristic that I noticed about Joshua is that when he knew there was an important part for him to play in the work of the Lord, it says that "Joshua rose early in the morning" (Joshua 3:1; 6:12,15; 7:16). Joshua was not lazy or slothful. He did not lay in bed for most of the day. He knew he must rise early to get the task at hand accomplished.

The following are several scriptures pertaining to laziness:

The hand of the diligent will rule, but the slothful will be put to forced labor (Proverbs 12:24).

The slothful (lazy) man does not catch his game or roast it once he kills it, but the diligent man gets his precious possessions (Proverbs 12:27).

The way of the sluggard is overgrown with thorns, (it pricks, lacerates and entangles him), but the way of the righteous is raised like a highway (Proverbs 15:19).

He who is loose and slack in his work is brother to him who is a destroyer and he who does not use his endeavors to heal himself is brother to him who commits suicide (Proverbs 8:9).

The desire of the slothful kills him, for his hands refuse to labor (Proverbs 12:25).

The sluggard says, there is a lion outside! I shall be slain in the streets! (Proverbs 22:13)

I went by the field of the lazy man, and by the vineyard of the man void of understanding; and behold, it was all grown over with thorns, and nettles were covering its face, and its stone wall was broken down. Then I beheld and considered it well; I looked and received instruction. Yet a little sleep, a little slumber, a little folding of the hands to sleep—so shall your poverty come as a robber, and your want as an armed man (Proverbs 24:30-34).

The word "slothful" in the *Strong's Concordance*, means to be slack, to lean idly, to be a sluggard. One word for slothful is "indolence," which carries the meaning of having the lifestyle or habit of being lazy. People who are lazy and sleep late, as a lifestyle, will be dull of hearing, feeling, understanding, energy, or vision.

The scripture in Proverbs 22:13 where the lazy man sees the lion outside and then states he will die in the streets is a picture of a person who sees an obstacle but has no idea how to get around or do away with the obstacle. There is no vision, no plans, or courage to even try. We need to arise, get the weapons we need, and go kill the lion in the street. Now is the time to get on with our lives!

Joshua arose early in the morning. He was a man who had been directed by the Lord how to subdue the enemy. He wanted to get started. He was excited about receiving his inheritance and becoming all that God had called him to do and to be. We cannot sit around waiting for someone to do for us what God tells us to do. We need to get up and begin somewhere with what we have. Our beginning will be small, but God will bring the increase as we follow Him in active obedience. We just have to give Him something to work with!

Joshua took time to get into the Lord's presence and hear what He had to say. When he heard the commands, he obeyed and went to the people to give them God's commands. The people then had to choose to act and obey in pursuing their destiny and possessing their possession! It is the same with us. We need to choose to rise and fulfill our divine destiny and be everything that God has designed us to be!

Sanctify Yourselves

In telling Israel to prepare themselves, Joshua was speaking of their natural needs, but he also told them to "sanctify themselves." The word "sanctify" means to consecrate or to cleanse. The people were told to separate and cleanse themselves from anything that was unclean and give themselves wholly to the Lord. They were commanded to a personal cleansing and to be diligent in their preparation.

The following are some scriptures dealing with cleansing and preparing ourselves.

I will wash my hands in innocence, so I will go about Your altar, O, Lord (Psalms 26:6).

I desire therefore that men pray everywhere, lifting up holy hands without wrath and doubting (I Timothy 2:8).

...let us draw near with a true heart in full assurance of faith, having our hearts sprinkled from an evil conscience and our bodies washed with pure water (Hebrews 10:22).

Therefore, having these promises, beloved, let US cleanse ourselves from all filthiness of the flesh and spirit, perfecting holiness in the fear of God (II Corinthians 7:1).

And everyone who has this hope purifies himself, just as He is pure (I John 3:3).

Draw near to God and He will draw near to you. Cleanse your hands you sinners and purify your hearts you double-minded (James 4:8).

Come out from among the world, and be ye separate, saith the Lord (II Corinthians 6:17).

We tend to look at the command of separation and holiness in the Word as a choice,. But it is not a choice, it is a command. If we are going to have the presence of God in our midst, if we are going to hear from Him, and have His manifested presence in our lives, we must live holy, separated lives! The word "separate" in the Greek means "to set boundaries and convictions." How many of us truly live by convictions? How many set boundaries and will not cross the line no matter what it may cost them?

Joshua 3:5 says the reason they were to sanctify themselves was that the next day the Lord Himself would work wonders among them. Do we not experience more of the presence, power and wonders of God today because we have not diligently prepared and cleansed ourselves? Do we live too much like the world? Holiness is a command in the Word of the Lord.

CHAPTER SIX

FOLLOW THE ARK

Yet there shall be a space between you and it, about two thousand cubits by measure. Do not come near it, that you may know the way by which you must go, for "You have not passed this way before" (Joshua 3:4).

The Ark of God held the law of God, which represents the Word of the Lord. It also represented the power and presence of God! They were told to stay 2000 cubits behind it or about one-half mile. I wondered why they needed to stay so far back. Since the Ark represents the presence and the Word of God, I would want to walk as close as possible to it.

When I asked God for the reason, He began to reveal the following to me:

• We must always remember we are sinners saved by His grace. Except for the grace of God, we would be eternally separated from His holy presence.

• The Mercy Seat was over the Ark between the Cherubim. It served as a lid. Except for this Mercy Seat, we would have only judgment for our sins. But Jesus Christ became our Mercy Seat and when God looks at us, He sees Jesus, our Mediator, between His holiness and my sin.

• As Christians, we are to keep our eyes focused upon Him. Hebrews 12:2 says "...looking unto Jesus, the author and finisher of our faith."

• Christ is high above us. He is greatly, immeasurably superior to us (Col. 1:18).

• We must not have unholy familiarity before the Lord. There must always be reverence, respect and awe of who He is.

• We cannot keep Him to ourselves. There is a world that must see who He is.

• He has already satisfied and obtained our inheritance through Jesus. Now we must go and possess or possession.

Under the Old Testament, the people of God and the priesthood went through a ceremonial cleansing, which was a type of the New Testament moral and internal cleansing. We must be cleansed, sanctified, and set apart for the worship and service of the Lord. He is holy and we must be holy (I Peter 1:16). Through Jesus Christ, it is possible for us to live clean, separated holy lives. If this was too hard for us to do, He would not have commanded us to be holy, as He is holy!

Who Carries the Ark?

The Ark is representative of the Word, power, and presence of God. In Joshua 3:6, He told the priests to take up the ark and cross over before the people. Up to this point, the sons of Kohath had carried the Ark. Now the priests were appointed to carry the Ark of the Lord. In the New Testament, we are called the Priesthood of Believers.

> But, you are a chosen generation, a royal priesthood, a holy nation, His own special people. That you may proclaim the praises of Him who has called you out of darkness into His marvelous light (Peter 2:9).

> ...and from Jesus Christ, the faithful witness, the firstborn from the dead, and the ruler over the kings of the earth. To Him who loved us, and washed us from our sins, in His own blood, and has made us kings and priests to His God and Father, to Him be glory and dominion forever and ever. Amen (Revelation 1:5-6).

The Old Testament speaks of a priesthood which God called to carry out the duties of worship and service on behalf of the people. The Levitical priesthood was responsible for carrying the furnishings and utensils of the House of the Lord. Once a year, the High Priest could go into the Holy of Holies, where the Shekinah glory dwelt.

In the New Testament, because of the death, burial, and resurrection of Jesus Christ, we have been made a kingdom of priests. We are now called to carry the Word, power, and presence of God, wherever we go. If we are going to perform our duties of worship and service, we must live clean, separated lives.

> Who may ascent to the hill of the Lord? Or who

may stand in His Holy Place? He who has clean hands and a pure heart, who has not lifted up his soul to an idol, nor sworn deceitfully (Psalms 24:3-4).

These verses speak of going into His presence (ascending) and dwelling in His presence (standing). There are those who move in and out of His presence, but I believe in these last days, there is a people who are hungering after God as never before. They long to dwell in His presence and stay separated unto Him; and wherever they go, they carry the presence of the Lord with them, just as did the priests of the Old Testament carried the Ark of the Covenant.

He Will Perform Wonders

Joshua told Israel that God would do wonders among them. The requirement for them to experience the power and presence of God was that they had to be prepared and separated unto Him. They believed what Joshua said and began to obey the commands of their leaders. They were full of faith and courage. Joshua and his people exercised total obedience when it came time to move into their inheritance.

I believe that there is a people who are coming forth with the "spirit of Joshua" upon them today! They are not moved by what they see, hear, or what obstacle they come against. They know their God and they live by faith in every word He says. They have laid down their lives and walk in obedience to His Word at any cost. They are rising up and will take the land that God has promised to them. They are going to possess their possession!

Be About Our Father's Business

We must first hear the Word of the Lord, spend time in His presence, and then obey all that His Word says. As the priesthood of believers, we are to carry the presence of the Lord with us everywhere we go. We are moving into new territory as His Church. There has never been a day like this. We have never passed this way before. We have never lived in a day where there is so much fear—people afraid to drink our water, ride in trains, airplanes, buses, or subways because of the possibility there is a terrorist lurking nearby. Two-thirds of Americans polled say they believe a terrorist attack could come at any moment, anywhere. There is a fear of chemical and biological warfare. We must display the spirit of Joshua and listen to God and not to the fear that controls so many. We must not be shaken by what we see, but only moved by the Word of God and what He says.

As we walk in obedience to His commands, He shall do wonders for us and through us, but we must keep ourselves prepared in His Word and in prayer, cleansed and separated from the defilement of the world. We must be a people of faith and courage, believing He will do what He says. Like the early church of the Book of Acts, we must have an anointing of boldness to speak forth truth!

that each of you should know how to possess his

own vessel in sanctification and honor...
(I Thessalonians 4:4).

It is time that we take personal responsibility for our natural and spiritual lives and be diligent and busy about the Father's business. We must let go of pettiness and selfishness and begin to both do and be the church that our heavenly Father dreams about and has purposed us to be!

CHAPTER SEVEN

THE SERVANT'S HEART

One day my mother and I were riding along in the car. We were each buried deep in our own thoughts until I broke the silence with this statement, "Mom, I can't stand people!" She glanced at me and sat quietly for a few seconds. Then with compassionate sternness in her voice she asked me, "Diane, do you want to work in the ministry?" Without hesitation I replied, "Yes." Then she spoke a simple, yet profound statement, which began to change my way of thinking. She said, "Diane, the ministry is all about people. Who will you minister to?"

I wanted to defend my statement, maybe even change it. But how could I? For a few minutes there was silence. Then I said, "Mom, I didn't mean what I said. It just came out wrong. You know what I mean." But I knew deep inside, I did mean it. I didn't trust people and I looked at them as potential for pain. I knew my mom was right. I had to have a heart change.

When we returned home, I went into my bedroom because I wanted to be alone to think about what just happened. There were places in me that needed healing. I truly cried out to the Lord. I asked Him to please help me. I said to Him, "If you really have called me, I want

Your heart of compassion. I want to see with Your eyes, hear with Your ears, and feel with Your heart." I didn't know the magnitude of what I was praying!

Looking back, I remember times when our family would have to delay or cancel our vacations because someone needed my dad and mom. One time in particular, we were about to embark on a much anticipated vacation. Our parents sent us to bed very early because the next morning at dawn, we would be leaving to enjoy a week of fun. The sun came piercing through my window, and I awakened to the warmth of its rays. What was going on? Why had no one awakened us earlier? I ran to my parent's room. My dad was putting on a suit and tie. These were not vacation clothes.

I asked what was going on. He told me that an elderly man in our church had passed away during the night. We would have to wait until a later time to go on vacation because the family needed him and my mother. I didn't say anything, but I was feeling plenty. I ran to my brothers' rooms and woke them up. I told them we would not be leaving and the reason why. My tone was less than gentle! I was mad and I wanted them to be angry too.

About that time, my parents came into the room. They heard every word and they were not pleased! My dad looked at me and said, "Diane, these people have lost someone they loved very much. Their hearts are breaking. I am their pastor. Our lives are spent touching, loving, and ministering to people, whatever their need. Don't you think you are being selfish? I want you to stop and think about what you are saying and feeling!"

With that, he walked out of the room. I was going to try to defend myself, but what was the use? I knew he was right. I went into my room and sat in silence, pondering this whole situation. I knew that what my dad said was the truth. How many times would this happen? How much of our lives would be given away? I remember hearing the telephone ring all hours of the night so many times, and plans being changed because someone needed my parents.

What was it that guided my dad? What caused him to pray and study the Word hour upon hour? What caused him to embrace men that didn't care when he spoke to them? What was it that caused him and my mom to give of themselves so completely when it seemed that most of the people didn't realize the depth of what they gave?

What kept my mom on her knees crying out for Dad, myself, my brothers and others? What was bigger than losing sleep, delaying vacations, financial pressures, and being on call 24 hours a day, seven days a week?

Little did I realize that I would embark on a journey that would lead me to the answer. The answer would come through life's process of daily experience and teach me the one principle that would forever govern my life.

Take Your Shoes Off

In Joshua 3, the Lord instructed him to appoint twelve men, one from each tribe of Israel, to carry the Ark over the Jordan River. There was a pattern that had to be followed to secure the victory for the children of Israel.

> *And it shall come to pass, as soon as the soles of the feet of the priests, who bear the ark of the Lord, the Lord of all the earth, shall rest in the waters of the Jordan, that the waters of the Jordan shall be cut off, and they shall stand as a heap* (Joshua 3:13).

In the Bible, the term "soles of the feet" represent servanthood. In this particular passage, the priests were to come to the water and stand at its edge for hours while the multitude passed over. Verse fifteen tells us that it was harvest time and that the Jordan, "overflows all its banks."

With the bulging and impassable river in front of them, they were commanded to go and stand in the edge of the Jordan. What a test of faith and obedience! To the carnal mind, this probably seemed senseless; standing in place, barefoot, hour upon hour, bearing the Ark.

We all go through times like this as we pursue our divine destiny. We have tried to obey to the best of our ability, yet we find ourselves in circumstances that are too deep and too wide to pass through. We come to the edge of our "Jordan," which is an impossible situation to overcome. It is here, in this place of seeming impossibility, that we learn to rely upon the wisdom and direction of our sovereign Lord.

Everyone who is called to work in the ministry will be tested and proven. There will be times when what we are going through and what we are asked to do does not make any sense. It will seem to our carnal reasoning that there has to be a better way. I have learned, by the process of testing and time, there is no better way than God's way. God not only looks at what we do, but He will test the motives of our heart.

The Training Process

When my husband and I were first married, we felt that the Lord wanted us to help his parents in the church they were pastoring. My mother-in-love (that's her pet name), taught about 25 teenagers in Sunday School. She asked me if I would teach the class because she had other responsibilities that needed her attention. so I agreed. The first couple of Sundays went great. I was excited, and it seemed the kids were, too. On the third Sunday, I walked into the class, my Bible and my notes tucked under my arm, and a spring in my prideful step!

Only one young man was sitting in the back. It was fifteen minutes until class started, so I waited for the others to arrive. Twenty minutes later no one else had come in. I walked out and said to my mother-in-love, "There is only one boy in the class this morning. We will just go out and sit in the auditorium. I don't want to embarrass him." She looked at me and said, "Diane, you go in that classroom, and you teach like you were teaching 100 kids." I couldn't believe what I was hearing. I knew there was no arguing with her so I turned around and walked into the class and told the young man "it's just us today."

I began to teach him. He never once looked up, not once! I thought, "This is ridiculous!" When class was over, he stood up, smiled at me, and then left. He was back the next Sunday, along with other students, but he left a few months later and I did not see him for some time. When I finally did see him, the first thing he said was, "Do you remember that Sunday morning when I was the only one in your class?" I told him, "Yes, I remember." He told me he had never forgotten that day. It meant a lot to him that I would stand and teach like that, when he was the only one there. He hugged me and walked off.

Immediately I thought of the words that my mother-in-love said to me when I walked out of the class that Sunday morning. "Diane, I know you don't understand why I had you teach today, but honey, the Lord doesn't care about the number we teach, He only looks at our submission and faithfulness to what He has called us to!" What a life lesson!

Why do we despise small beginnings? The small beginnings, with all of the frustrations and the disappointments, are part of the process that God takes us through to teach us character, to be able to reflect His image.

Faithfulness

His lord said to him, "Well done good and faithful servant; you were faithful over a few things, I will make you ruler over many things. Enter into the joy of your lord" (Matthew 25:21).

The greatest principle that we can learn and develop in our lives is that of faithfulness. This does not happen over night. It is during this training process that we learn to be patient and develop the stick-to-it mentality, because we understand others are depending on us.

As the priests stood at the brink of the Jordan with the swelling waters all around them, bearing the Ark of the Covenant, they were examples of leaders in the Body of Christ. The priests bore His presence and the congregation was privileged to come near to His presence. The priesthood bore the heaviest load. There are times when the load feels heavy, but I have learned to fall on my knees and cry out to my Father.

I am sure their shoulders grew tired as they stood in the place of their destiny. At times, they would have loved to trade places with someone else who was already moving on to bigger and better things.

They became hungry and thirsty. Their minds journeyed to a land flowing with milk and honey. They could have easily laid down the Ark and walk over to the other side. They were tired, but there was something on the inside of each of them. They had been given a command by their leader. They had a destiny to fulfill. They were servants of the Most High God. They would stay in their place until all of the people were safe!

Many years earlier, Moses was on the backside of the desert, reflecting on when he had killed an Egyptian trying to protect his people. His own people wanted him dead when all that he had wanted to do was to help. His motives had been so misunderstood, and he had to run for his very life. What Moses perceived about this wilderness experience and what God knew, were totally opposite. One day after forty years, God appeared in a burning bush and said, "Take your shoes off, Moses, for you are on holy ground." God was saying, "Moses, I am here. I am calling you to lead My people out of bondage.

I have heard their cries. It is time to set them free! You are My servant. As long as you maintain the attitude of serving My people, My presence will go with you. Moses, just like this burning bush, you will never be consumed by the responsibilities of the call, as long as you dwell in My presence."

In Joshua chapter one, God said to Joshua, "Every place the sole of your foot treads upon, I have given to you." In other words, "Every place you maintain the heart of a servant, a broken and humble heart, I will bless you and I will prosper you." I have often heard it said that attitude determines outcome. The attitude of our heart determines our victory.

God could have divided the river without the help of the priests, but they could not have divided it without Him. We can do nothing of ourselves. It is in Him we live and move and have our being. Our very existence depends upon Him. We are privileged that He took the time to create us and breathe His breath into us to give us His life!

In Joshua 5:13-15, Joshua had just led the children of Israel over the Jordan River onto dry land. He had been exalted as a leader in the eyes of the people. God had been true to His Word. After they crossed over, the Lord told Joshua to circumcise all the sons of Israel, since none of them (except for Joshua and Caleb) had been circumcised yet . Circumcision was a sign of the covenant between God and His people. It was a cutting away of the flesh. Before we move on into the next level of our purpose, we must allow the Word of God to cut away the fleshly areas of our lives. To be His servant, the selfishness has to go! Hebrews 4:12 says,

For the word of God is living and powerful, sharper than any two-edged sword, 'piercing' even to the joints and marrow, and is a discerner of the thoughts and intents of the heart.

Before they were going to leave their camp, Joshua went to investigate Jericho. As any good leader getting ready to go into battle, he went to look at the wall, determining his best plan of action. We know that the Lord fights our battles, but we must also be wise and responsible to our duties.

"He lifted up his eyes and saw a Man who was standing in front of him." It seems that after he viewed the wall, he prepared to seek the Lord. When he lifted up his eyes, he saw a Man standing in front of him with His sword drawn. Joshua did not realize who it was and asked Him, "Are you on our side or are you against us?" The Man responded, "No, I am the Commander of the army of the Lord."

He was inferring that there were no sides. "I AM Jehovah. Take your shoes off, Joshua. You are on holy ground." This was exactly what the Lord had said to Moses when he first called him. When God begins to move you from one level of service to another, He will reveal Himself to you in a new way. Before we can be used by Him, we must know Him through personal revelation.

Now he was saying to Joshua what God had said to Moses. Joshua's response was to fall on his face. It was a response of humility and worship. He obeyed the Lord by taking off his sandals and then he asked, "What does my Lord say to His servant?" Here again we see a picture of the presence of the Lord, producing humility and creating an attitude of servanthood. When the manifest presence of God truly comes, we will fall on our knees, in awe of His holiness!

Isaiah 40:31 says "But those who wait on the Lord shall renew their strength; they shall mount up with wings like eagles, they shall run and not be weary, they shall walk and not faint." The Strong's Concordance says that the word "wait" has a two-fold meaning. In this verse, the Hebrew meaning would be to bind together, to expect, gather together, look patiently, tarry; wait for, Wait on, or wait upon (serve).

The 1828 *Webster's Dictionary* says that the word "wait" means to attend as a servant, to perform services for, to attend to, to be ready to serve, to obey, to accompany with submission or respect. We must gather together and wait in His presence, spending time with Him, staying long enough to allow Him to speak to our hearts. Prayer is a two-way street. Most of the time we do all of the talking. We plead and beg, and tell Him all about what we want, and then we leave Him before He can speak.

> *For though I am free from all men, I am, myself a SERVANT to all, that I might win the more, and to the Jews I became as a Jew, that I might win Jews; to those who are under the law, as under the law, that I might win those who are under the law; to those who are without law, as without law, (not being without law toward*

God, but under law toward Christ), that I might win those who are without law, to the weak I became weak, that might win the weak. I have become all things to all men, that I might by all means save some. Now, this I do for the gospel's sake, that I may be a partaker of it with you (I Corinthians 9:19-23)

In these verses, Apostle Paul is saying that without sinning or violating any moral law of the Bible, he would go anywhere to any length into the world of any person, if it would lead them to salvation. He says, "I have made myself a 'servant' to all." You cannot pray for an attitude of serving; you must make a *choice* to serve. You cannot pray for servanthood, nor can you pray for humility—both are a matter of choice.

I Peter 5:5 "Likewise you younger people, submit yourselves to your elders. Yes, all of you be submissive to one another and be clothed with humility, for God resists the proud, but gives grace to the humble." We must choose to put on humility, just like we put on our clothing. The way we dress ourselves is what everyone sees. If we are clothed with humility, everyone will know.

The Humility of Jesus

For who is greater, he who sits at the table, or he who serves? Is it not he who sits at the table? But, I am among you, as the One who serves (Luke 22:27).

63

In Matthew 20:28 Jesus said, "I did not come to be served, I came to serve." Jesus speaks of Himself as a servant to all men, everywhere. As we wait in His presence, and walk in obedience to His Word, we will be partakers of His divine nature (II Peter 1:4).

A tree can only grow with the life that was in the seed from which it first came. In understanding this truth, we can look at the fallen nature of Adam in Genesis, and then look at the second Adam of the New Testament, Jesus Christ. We can easily see the need for a nature change, in and by the redemptive work of Calvary through Jesus.

Satan was cast out of heaven because of the pride that consumed him. He desired to be worshiped like God. His nature was the nature of pride. He deceived Eve into disobeying God's command, not to eat of the tree of knowledge of good and evil. Eve yielded her will to the potential that she could be as God, able to know good and evil. Pride entered into her very life.

She disobeyed and pride entered, destroying her humility and dependence upon God. Referring back to the above truth, everything in life comes from a seed. The life of the seed that we come from is the only life inside of us. We were born with the corrupted nature of Eve inside us. All of the world's evil has its beginning in the sin of pride—wars, jealousies, unforgiveness, bitterness, and selfishness. As a result, we need to be changed! We have to have a change in our nature, and it only comes through the redemptive work of Calvary.

That is why Jesus came—to change us from the inside out. He came so that He could give us a new nature, the very nature of Christ. We need to study the nature of God, the life that was revealed through Christ, while He was here on earth.

> *Let this mind be in you which was also in Christ Jesus, who being in the form of God, did not consider it robbery to be equal with God, but made Himself of no reputation, taking the form of a bondservant, and coming in the likeness of men, being found in appearance a man, humbled Himself, and became obedient to the point of death, even the death of the cross* (Philippians 2:5-8)

He emptied Himself and became a man and a servant to all men. He humbled Himself and became obedient to death. He humbled Himself, and God highly exalted Him.

> He is the eternal love, humbling itself, clothing itself in the garb of meekness and gentleness, to win and to serve and to save us. Even in the midst of the throne, He is the meek and lowly Lamb of God (Andrew Murray).

In John 15, Jesus calls Himself the true vine, and His Father, the vinedresser. We are the branches, connected to the life of the vine. Humility and servanthood are the root of the vine, therefore this nature has to be seen in every branch, every leaf and in all of its fruit. Humility encompasses all that Jesus is and does. The strength of our spiritual life totally depends on us being clothed in the humility of His divine nature.

The book of Romans opens with these words, "Paul, a bondservant of Jesus Christ." The books of Ephesians, Philippians, Titus, and Philemon all open with a salutation of servanthood from the Apostle Paul. James greets us calling himself a bondservant of God and of the Lord Jesus Christ. Peter also calls himself a bondservant of Christ.

When Peter was martyred, because of the Gospel he preached, he requested that his executioners hang him upside down on the cross because he did not deserve to die as his Savior did. What humility! What servanthood!

In John 6:38, Jesus said, "I came down from heaven, not to do my own will." And in John 8:50 Jesus said, "I seek not mine own glory." These words speak to us of the deeper part of Christ's life. This is why the Father could work His redemptive plan through Him. Christ was willing to become nothing, so that God could become all. He gave everything up—His will, His glory, and His power—so that His Father could work through Him. He did not seek glory for Himself. He came with a mission, to do the will of the Father!

If we are going to have anything, do anything, or be anything, we must clothe ourselves in humility so that we can lay down our lives to serve others. After so many times of going from "glory TO glory," and living in the "to" area of life, I finally understand the cancelled vacations and postponed plans. My parents had crossed the line. They were no longer living to themselves and their own comfort; their hearts were given away to the will of the Father.

Like Apostle Paul said, "It is no longer I that live, but it is Christ that lives in me." A true servant of God, whether man or woman, has to be clothed in humility and be willing to give his life away for the sake of others coming to Christ. Paul was willing to do or be anything, (without sinning), in order to bring salvation to those who were without hope.

There is a line you cross to do the will of the Father, and once you cross it, you do not look back. The Apostle Paul in Philippians 3:13-14, speaks of forgetting the things behind—all the trials, the hurts, the disappointments and grief—to press on toward the prize of the upward call of God in Christ Jesus.

Personal Testimony

In closing this chapter, I want to share a personal testimony with you. It is a life lesson that changed me so deeply, and I am truly thankful.

In October of 1993, my mother-in-love was diagnosed with breast cancer. When you hear that word, cancer, you want to run away from all that you know could happen. None of us, her husband, son, daughter, grandchildren, or sisters wanted to believe it. Not her, a beautiful, vibrant, strong, anointed woman of God. No way! This could not be! After a while, when our hearts settled, she told us to stop with all the emotionalism and instructed us that we were to stand on the Word of God with her, for her total healing. That was that! That's how she was!

One Saturday afternoon, I went to their home next door. Mom Mullins, without warning, asked me if I wanted to see or touch the lump in her breast. I said I would look at it, but no way could I touch it. I cringed and made an untimely, selfish statement and went home. I realized later that she needed someone to share with her in the changes that her body was going through. Only another woman could understand how it feels to have this disease attack this part of your body. I ran when I should have stayed.

During the night, God woke me up and asked me these questions; "Why did you act like that today? You were very immature and selfish. What you did not want to touch is in her body. She lives with it every day. I want you to go to her tomorrow and give your life away! Tell her that you will be there for her no matter what she may face. You will stand with her for healing, and be whatever she needs you to be. Tell her that you will never allow her to lose her dignity. You are her hand-maiden for as long as she needs you. I will give you the strength to do all I have asked of you."

I am not writing this as if I was, or am now, someone great! Just the opposite. Selfish pieces of my life had to be cut away, to fashion and create a servant's heart. Like most, I saw my comfort first, others second. And like most other people, I didn't realize this about myself. God was going to show me what it meant to lay down my life.

The following day, I went to their house. I asked her to sit down, that I had something I needed to say. After I told her all that I felt I needed to, she laid her head down on the table and began to cry. Finally she looked up at me, and we both smiled. There were not really a lot of words needed. We both knew that day that God had bonded us together forever. For the first time, I wondered if maybe we weren't feeling what Naomi and Ruth did when Ruth, the daughter-in-law, pledged herself to Naomi.

One day, she asked us, the family, to gather because she had come to a decision. She told us that she did not want to take any treatments. She had faith that God would heal her, but if for some reason He wanted her by His side, she would trust Him. She was at peace with her decision. She made it clear there was not to be any negative talk, and we were all to live our lives as normally as possible.

After some months went by, the tumor began to grow larger and the pain was becoming almost unbearable. The only medication she would take was Tylenol 3. Every day I went to her side to check on her and to see what I could do. I felt so responsible for her and wanted so much to relieve her pain and discomfort. I was experiencing compassion I had never felt before.

One day a friend came to take me shopping. She felt I needed a break and reluctantly I agreed to go. We had been gone about an hour when I called home. My mind was not really on shopping! I asked my mom-in-love how she was doing and she told me fine, not to worry. It was hard to do that. Our lives had become so intertwined. I didn't want to be gone from her for very long.

She was saying she was doing okay, but I could hear the pain. I could hear that she needed me, so I went back to her. From that day on, I stayed with her most of the time, going home just long enough to check on and take care of my own family, then I would return to her side to do what I could.

If I ever saw a picture of true servanthood, it was in my father-in-love. He was at her side day and night. He would sit and hold her, praying, quoting scriptures, gently loving her, more than his own flesh. Many times I would go into his office and he would be sitting, holding his Bible with tears gently flowing down his face. We would cry together and then return to her side.

One day he was going up to her room, when he stopped halfway up the stairs and just laid there. He was so exhausted. He had to rest for a moment. That very night, I watched him go to the pulpit of the church, and preach to his congregation. Over and over he did this. No matter how tired he was or how painful the day had been, he remained faithful to pastor his congregation.

One day she called me to her side and taught me how to put her makeup on her, especially her lipstick. She told me when anyone would come to visit, she didn't want to look sick. She made me promise to always make sure she had makeup on and her hair styled. She loved clothes, jewelry and makeup. She knew how to shop and get the best for less!

I promised her I would do that for her. I remembered at the beginning of all of this, I had told her I would never let her lose her dignity, and I meant it.

There were so many sleepless nights. Her pain was almost unbearable. We would sit with her, reading the Bible, singing or just quietly talking about the goodness of the Lord.

A little more than a year from the day she received

the diagnosis, she did not leave the house any more. Then, after a while, she didn't come downstairs again. She stayed in bed or sat in a chair in her bedroom. The pain had become almost more than she could bear, and breathing was very hard for her. I had never before felt so helpless, and many times I silently screamed through the night.

I was learning what it means to lay down your life for someone else. Eventually everything had to be done for her. A few days before she passed away, she began to set her focus heavenward. The last night of her life here on earth, she asked me to come close. I laid my head on her lap. With all the strength she could muster, she lifted her hand to stroke my head. She told me to take up the slack. I asked her what she wanted me to do. She said, "Diane, nobody really wants to die, but I am tired. Step into the place where I will no longer be able to stand and love people and touch their lives."

She asked me and another friend who was there, along with my father-in-love, to sing "As the Deer Panteth for the Water." A wonderful peace settled in her room. She went into a deep sleep, and the next morning, God brought her to His side while all of heaven stood at attention.

I finally understood what it meant to give your whole self to someone else. There is a place of serving that embraces your heart, and the only time you find fulfillment is when you are serving another. It is not about me or my comfort. Life in Jesus is becoming whatever we need Him to be, to all people, so that we can give them the love of Christ and lead them to His love.

Just like my own parents, my mother and father-in-love had also crossed the line. They were giving their lives away to serve others, even when they were in need themselves. In the midst of their own battles, their concern was for the Lord's body and all those who did not know Him.

There is no fear in love; but, perfect love casts out fear, because fear involves torment. But he who fears has not been made in perfect love (I John 4:18).

This verse has been made so clear to me. The word perfect means "mature." The meaning of this passage is what both sides of my family lived. To help or minister to someone else, will many times feel uncomfortable, but when love is perfect, or mature, it doesn't matter what you go through, you will do whatever you can to help those in need and make their lives better.

For a better understanding, imagine yourself walking down the street and suddenly you see that a house is on fire. You run to where the fire is and when you get closer, you can see that a child is screaming for help from a second story window. Without hesitation, you run into the house and save the child.

This is a picture of mature love. You would run into that burning inferno without a thought of what it could cost you in order to save someone else. That is what Christ did for us when He came to earth. That is how we must live, partaking of His divine nature.

I have seen this principle in action and I know it

works. There is something greater than my own blessings or comfort. It is being broken and poured out for the sake of others. I thank God for the examples of "servanthood" throughout my life that now, by His grace, govern my life!

Have you given yourself away? Are you still holding onto parts of yourself that it's time to let go of? Look for someone to minister to. Touch someone's life in the same way that someone touched your life. There is so much joy in waiting on the Lord and serving others!

CHAPTER EIGHT

GLORY TO GLORY

To everything there is a season, a time for every purpose under heaven (Ecclesiastes 3:1).

Several years ago I was going through one of the greatest trials of my life. Nothing was going the way I had always dreamed it would. Despair gripped my soul. I really wondered if I would ever laugh again.

One morning I was looking out my living room window. It was a cold, snowy, dull gray morning. A wooded area lined the backyards of the houses across the street. I thought to myself, "Those trees are so dull and lifeless. They look just like I feel."

Immediately the Holy Spirit spoke to me and said, "No, my child. You are wrong. There is life! You cannot see it, but underground there is ceaseless activity. The roots are preparing to manifest life. There is more life now than in the spring when the buds come forth, or in the season of summer, when everything is plush and green. When you see all of the beautiful colors in the fall season, that really signals death, and deep in the earth, the cycle of life starts again."

Immediately I took what the Lord had just spoken to me and saw where I had grown through each season, as I learned how to submit to my heavenly Father. I began to see that our lives evolve around seasons of change. Uncomfortable as they are, the changes, the pain, and the tests move us from one level of maturity to the next. Second Corinthians 3:18 says that we are being transformed from glory to glory into the image of the Lord.

When we reach a level of glory—maturity in Christ—and win a great battle, it seems almost before we finish rejoicing, we find ourselves in another "to" area. Most of us, stay in the "to" area, more than the "glory" area. This is what life is all about, growing, changing, maturing, and being made into His likeness. This process does not happen overnight. Thank God for the "glory times," but we can't stop there. We have to move on!

If you are in a "to" area right now, don't lose heart. Rejoice! God is working something deep inside of you, preparing you for a glorious purpose in His kingdom. Many times what feels like the most painful experience of our lives are the times when we changed the most!

The Next Step

Joshua, as leader of Israel, found himself at this exact place. He was leading a new generation into their God-given inheritance. When they came to their first major obstacle, the Jordan River with its overflowing banks, God gave him direction for their victory. The Israelites were ready to possess the Promised Land. God put them at this place for a purpose. He never brings us to a challenge except that there is a divine purpose in it.

After crossing the Jordan River, they camped in Gilgal and ate of the produce of the land. The next day verse 12 says, "Then the manna ceased." God had provided manna for them, six days a week during their wilderness journey. When they entered the land, God's provision would be through another means. He would still be their provider, just as He had always been, but now they would learn personal responsibility through plowing, planting, and watering the land, and then eating what the land provided by their hands. This was just one of many changes that they would go through, and each change brought a new challenge for them to meet and conquer.

Prior to taking Jericho, Joshua came face to face with the Lord, although Joshua did not recognize Him at first. Joshua asked Him whose side He was on. The Lord's reply was, "I AM," meaning there are no sides. "I AM the leader who will take you through to victory." Joshua's faith and confidence grew, realizing there was a mightier leader than himself who would lead this nation into battle.

Joshua and the Israelites trusted God's promise that He would drive out all their enemies. Their only responsibility was to follow in obedience to His every command. It is important to remember, that prior to going into the next level of glory or maturity, the enemy will come with his deceptive lies to get you off track. At the same time, the Lord will come to you with a fresh revelation of who He is. Joshua was visited by the Lord Himself prior to the battle of Jericho, and it filled him with renewed faith and fire for the battle.

Preparing for Battle

We now come to what could be the most interesting battle ever recorded—the fall of Jericho. The Canaanites occupied the land, so before Israel could possess the land of promise, they had to be destroyed. The Canaanites were devout idolaters. The city was full of enchanters, witches, and those who consulted with familiar spirits. Because of these abominations, the Lord said He would drive them out.

Jericho was on the border of the Promised Land, a key city to conquer. The walls around Jericho encircled about seven acres of land and made it a fortress that no enemy could get in. The fortress was small in proportion to the number of people who lived in the area, therefore, many of the people lived outside of the wall in the surrounding hillside. When they were threatened, the Canaanites living outside of the wall came inside for their safety.

When Israel reached Jericho, the people of Jericho had locked themselves within the walls because they had heard of all the miracles the Lord had performed for Israel. The gates to the city were tightly shut, and no one went in or out of the city, awaiting the approach of Israel's God.

The reputation of the living God preceded Israel, and the enemy did not want to fight! Although the Canaanites placed their hope in the strength and the height of the wall, they were afraid and uneasy. This heathen nation knew about the power and ability of the God of Israel. Did they really think a wall would protect them, or was this all they knew to do?

There is a difference between how we see ourselves and how others see us. This idolatrous, heathen nation had locked themselves behind the wall because they feared the Israelites' God. Are we at ease in Zion? Do we take for granted the love and mercy of God at the expense of His justice? Have we forgotten, or ever believed that He has all power and all authority in His hands? Do we forget that others see us connected to Him?

The Canaanite enemy was in awe of His mighty power! Are we? Do we see who He is, or are we just acquainted with what He does?

To Know Him

Psalms 103:7 says that Israel knew the *acts* of God, but Moses knew His *ways*. What is the difference? Apostle Paul wrote three-fourths of the New Testament, and at the end of his life, from the Philippian jail he cried, "Oh that I may know Him!" How could Paul say that? If anyone can know Christ, it seems he would have. Still, he knew there was a deeper place, a deeper revelation that he desired to experience.

To know God's acts is to know and see His actions. Israel saw the Red Sea parted by His mighty hand, and they were all witnesses to the ten plagues that caused Pharaoh to set them free. They were fed with manna from heaven, and their thirst was quenched with water from the rock. They knew His acts, but Moses knew His ways. Moses was close enough to Him to know His heart. He not only saw the acts of the Lord, but he knew why God performed them. He understood the purposes and motives of God's heart because he spent time with Him in the glory of His presence, as His friend.

As we walk in our purpose and are submitted to every command of the Lord, we can rest in His might and strength. He will fight our battles for us. Our responsibility is to listen and obey! Thus, God spoke to Joshua and gave him the plan for victory over Jericho! Stand still and see the salvation of the Lord!

The Divine Pattern

In chapter six, God revealed to Joshua the winning strategy, the divine direction that Israel needed to obey in order to be victorious in this battle. I believe that as we look at this unique strategy, we can see that it sets forth a pattern for us to understand, and govern our lives by.

> *And the Lord said to Joshua, "See! I have given Jericho into your hand, its king, and mighty men of valor. You shall march around the city, all you men of war; you shall go around the city once. This you shall do six days. And seven priests shall bear seven trumpets of rams' horns before the ark. But, the seventh day you shall march around the city seven times, and the priests shall blow the trumpets. It shall come to pass, when they make a long blast with the ram's horn, and when you hear the sound of the trumpet that all the people shall shout with a great shout; then the wall of the city will fall down flat. And the people shall go up, every man straight before him"* (Joshua 6:2-5).

Give God the Glory

The Lord's first word to Joshua was "See, I have given Jericho into your hand!" It is He who has won the victory. This statement was more than a faith building word from the Lord to show His bountiful provision for Israel. He was not going to allow fleshly pride to take the credit for the victorious battle of Jericho. The pride of flesh is running rampant today. It always has been and always will be. When our churches are growing, when we are in a high season of His presence and His glory, and excitement is mounting, we are prone to take the credit and the praise that belongs to God alone. This statement nullified any boasting of the flesh!

I am the vine, you are the branches. He who abides in Me, and I in him, bears much fruit; for without Me you can do nothing (John 15:5).

I am the Lord, that is My name; and My glory I will not give to another, nor my praise to carved images (Isaiah 42:8).

There is such a need today, for the boasting to stop. Everything good that happens in us, to us, and through us, is only from the Lord! We should not take any honor to ourselves. In Acts 12:23, King Herod was eaten up by worms because he did not give glory to God!

The primary focus of the instructions from the Lord to Joshua was, "I have given you victory. The battle has already been fought. I have blessed and prospered you, but, do not take the glory and give the credit to your-selves! The very breath that gives you life comes from My existence!"

There was a young man fresh out of Bible School. He was excited, ready to preach, and change the world! There was an elderly pastor who invited each graduate to preach their first sermon at his church. This young man was introduced, and with his head held high and his Bible under his arm, he quickly went to the pulpit. He was ready!

He opened his Bible and began. After only five min-utes he sat down. He was dejected and humiliated! He asked the older pastor, who was full of wisdom, what went wrong. The pastor's reply was, "Son if you would have gone up there like you came down, you would have came down like you went up!" What a simple revelation. Full of self, we try and fail. We must realize that it is God at work in us at all times!

We are to live our lives displaying His glory and His presence as the very essence of who we are and the reason for any victory in our lives. If we do not willingly give Him the glory and humble ourselves under His mighty hand, He will humble us! I choose to fall on the rock, before the rock falls on me.

CHAPTER NINE

YOU SHALL MARCH

When we look at the directions given by the Lord to Joshua, it makes us wonder. If the Lord had already secured the victory, why did He require the people to follow such intricate preparations for the overthrow of Jericho?

This scene illustrates the following principal which all of us must understand: God's revelation to us of His divine purpose and its certain completion does not do away with our responsibilities. God's divine design never is meant to promote inactivity in our lives.

God declared to Joshua that He had given them the land, but that declaration did not release them from their duties. We can be assured of victory when our efforts are in line with what the Lord says.

Just because something is spiritual does not mean we are to sit back and do nothing. Salvation is immediate, but after that, there are principles we have to learn, in order to mature and grow. Developing a relationship with Him is a priority! When we truly know Him, we will be keen to hear His voice and quickly obey!

My sheep hear My voice, I know them, and they follow Me (John 10:27).

The above verse is a promising guarantee to all who hear and obey, but, there is no word of encouragement given to those who do not heed His voice and instead choose to live a life of self-will and self-comfort.

In the natural realm there are principles for success. For example, we must eat to live and have strength in our bodies. It is the purpose of the earth to produce crops, but the only way they will grow is when the ground is prepared and the seed sown. Whose responsibility is it to break up the fallow ground? Who plants the seed? When the rains are held back, who waters the seed so that the harvest can come forth, in due season?

Proper Order

In the spiritual realm it is important to understand that we cannot do things our way, by our own methods. God has divine law and order, A great example of this is found in 1 Chronicles 13 when David expressed his desire to bring the Ark back to Jerusalem. David discussed the idea with his captains, leaders, and all the assembly, and the people readily agreed that the Ark should be brought back. (God's people had not been in possession of the Ark for 20 years because it had been stolen by the Philistines.)

This desire that David and Israel had for the Ark was indication of their growing hunger for God. David's desire was proper. He wanted the worship of Yahweh restored in Israel. He had a right motive but did not follow the proper order. Rather than first inquiring of the Lord, He went to the people and told them of his plan.

God had given specific directions in Exodus, concerning the making, and transporting of the Ark. It was never to be touched with flesh. The Ark represented God's holy presence. When David and his men went to retrieve the Ark, they decided upon their own method of transportation, rather than the divine pattern. They put the Ark on a cart, and when the animal pulling it stumbled on the rocky path, Uzzah put his hand on the Ark to keep it from falling, and he immediately died. Why? He just wanted to keep the Ark from falling. Our fleshly opinions would deem this action as unfair. But when we take a closer look at the reality of God's holiness and the divine pattern that Uzzah was well aware of, we can understand the outcome!

God had directed that the only ones who should carry the Ark were the Levites, and Uzzah was not a Levite. It was to be carried by poles, which went through golden rings, two on one side and two on the other. No flesh was to ever touch the presence of God. The Ark was holy, and God gave directions so that the holiness would never be defiled.

God's Word is forever settled and will not change. We cannot do things our way. We fail to ask for His direction, and then we ask Him to bless our efforts. Just as David and Uzzah were not left to follow their own devices, neither are we. They had been given specific instructions, and they were not followed. As a consequence, Uzzah lost his life. Each of us must obey the instructions of the Lord. His way *is* the best way. He is not a hard Taskmaster. His grace strengthens us to obey!

Having learned his lesson, later in 1 Chronicles 15

David proceeded the correct way and inquired of the Lord first for His directions on bringing the Ark of God back to Jerusalem.

Seven Days of Marching

Just as God had provided instruction for the return of the ark, He gave specific instruction for the taking of Jericho. All of Israel was commanded by God to walk around the wall of the city for seven days. The first six days they were to march once around the city. Seven priests were to blow seven trumpets, marching ahead of the ark. On the seventh day, they would march around Jericho seven times, and on the seventh time around, the priests were to blow the trumpets long and loud. As the trumpets blew, the people were to shout a great shout, and the wall of the city would then fall flat.

The number seven is mentioned several times in this narrative: seven priests, seven trumpets, seven days, and seven times around the city. As stated, the number seven represents maturity and the power of God. In Genesis, we read that God rested from His labors of creation on the seventh day. Israel entered into their inheritance on the seventh day. I believe this is a picture of Hebrews 4, when the "rest" of the Lord is described for us. It is a type of the new creation in Christ. We grow from glory to glory through the process of life lessons, then when we reach a certain level of maturity, we begin to enter into that "rest." This rest does not mean lack of activity. It is a spiritual maturity of trust in our heavenly Father, no matter what challenge we face.

The Lord had already given them the city, but there

were directions given to them that they had to obey to carry out their own responsibility to secure victory. The Ark of God held the Ten Commandments. It was representative of His presence, and also denoted that Israel now marched in agreement with Divine Law.

Only through obedience can we plan for success! As the Israelites walked in obedience to the divine pattern, their steps secured their victory. On the seventh day, the walls fell flat, and they captured the city! Their strict obedience to God's directions led to the ultimate defeat of their enemy!

God's Strength and Man's Weakness

Joshua called the priests to his side and told them to carry the Ark of the Covenant. Seven priests were to carry and blow seven trumpets of rams' horns, leading the ark. He gave them the Lord's specific instructions, and complete and immediate obedience was what was required of them. First they were to "take up the Ark of the Covenant," next, "bear seven trumpets of rams' horns," then, "go out in front of the Ark."

The term "ram's horns" is used five times in this chapter. There is a message to us in the use of this illustration. Silver trumpets were normally used in the camp of Israel, but in this passage God instructed them to use ram's horns. Ram's horns were the most raw and coarse material of the day. It represented an unfinished product. God chose this to show Israel's weakness and His strength. If someone was filled with pride in their accomplishments, they would not have wanted to use ram's horns! God shows us again that He will not share

His glory, and we must realize our dependency on Him. He chooses, what seems to us, the most inadequate way, so that His glory may be seen.

There was a two-fold reason for the priests to blow the trumpets. When the enemy heard the sound, they would be filled with fear; in contrast, the people of God who would be filled with faith and confidence.

But God has chosen the foolish things of the world to put to shame the wise, and God has chosen the weak things of the world to put to shame the things which are mighty; and the base things of the world and the things which are despised God has chosen, and the things which are not, to bring to nothing the things that are, that "no flesh" should glory in His presence (1 Corinthians 1:27).

...that, as it is written, "He who glories, let him glory in the Lord" (1 Corinthians 1:31).

CHAPTER TEN

NO TALKING, PLEASE

Marching day after day around the walls of Jericho, with no immediate or visible results, was an evident test of their obedience. The Ark leading the people and the continual blowing of the trumpets was representative of the power and purpose of worship. The hardest part of this test had to be the silence required of the people.

I walk (when weather permits) three miles a day. In about 40 minutes, at a quick steady pace, I am usually back home, guzzling water and taking deep breaths. This is not a scientific analogy, but at my pace, it would take about two hours to walk around the city. Can you imagine over a million people walking around the city, not speaking one word.

No matter how they felt, what they heard, or saw, they did not speak a word. There was no need for words. God Himself was about to speak in judgment over Jericho! It was not time for shallow excuses to one another or improper criticism of their leaders. As it says in Ecclesiastes 3:7, there is "a time to keep silence, and a time to speak."

The reason for Israel's 40-year journey in the wilderness was their murmuring. It is no wonder they were told to be silent. This command was a precaution against the negative speech of Israel. This should be a lesson to us all. When we are faced with situations out of our control or that seem too great for us, we should keep silent and not allow our words to be filled with unbelief. James tells us that life and death are in the power of the tongue. Our self-control can hasten the victory; our disobedience can prolong it!

In Matthew 12:37, Jesus says by our words we will be declared righteous, or we will be condemned. James 3:2 teaches us that when we are able to control our tongue, we are able to control our whole being. We cannot help what we see and hear, but, we can help and control what comes out of our mouths.

A few years back I was struggling with something I knew, wondering if I should tell someone else about it. I asked a friend what she thought. Her answer is worth repeating. She said, "Diane, before you tell something, or repeat something you have been told, ask yourself, 'What is the purpose of what I am going to say? Will what I am about to say bring about a positive result?'"

So many times we hurt others with our words. Most of the time we hurt the ones closest to us because we let down our guard. Scientists have found that light and sound travel at the same speed. If sound travels at 186,000 miles per second, then words that are spoken can travel forever. When the Holy Spirit reminds us of any hurtful words we have spoken, we need to call down their power, speak to those words to fall to the ground and die, rendering them void and ineffective.

The Reward of Obedient Faith

Let's visualize faith's course of obedience taken by the Israelites. Walking around the walled city of Jericho, once a day for six days brought jeering from the Canaanites, as they watched from high upon the wall. Israel, however, kept marching, without one sound of murmuring coming out of their mouths.

For six days there was no divine intervention. The walls stood as firm as ever. The Israelites kept up their pace, and one more time, one more day, they walked the designed path to victory. They walked out to the wall on the seventh day and began their march. The heat was exhausting; the path was rocky.

One trip around the wall took almost two hours, then seven times around the wall would have taken each of them about eight hours. They became tired and hungry. It seemed they were making fools of themselves in front of the Canaanites. They walk one, two, three times around, nothing happens. They continue, without one word spoken. They walk on, four, five, six, and then they take a deep breath. One more time around. The priests blow the trumpets, and Joshua says, "Shout for the Lord has given you the city!"

The seventh walk around was complete. Although the silence took much faith and obedience, the shout took even greater faith to obey. After all the silence, they were supposed to shout, while the wall was still standing! It is easy for us to shout *after* the victory! To shout *before* the victory is seen is an act of faith.

The priests blew their trumpets, shattering the silence. The people gave a great shout, and the walls begin to crumble and fall flat! As soon as the walls fell, all of Israel ran into the city. All the people—men, women, young and old—the oxen, sheep, and donkeys, every living being in the city, was utterly destroyed by the sword! God had given them the city, and their responsibility was to do it His way, in faithful obedience!

Many Christians make the mistake of assuming that faith is passive, defined as merely resting on the promises of God. Faith is not only believing in His Word, but faith is actively obeying what His Word says to do.

When the Israelites obeyed God's commands and walked around the wall of Jericho, they put themselves in harm's way. They did not have swords or spears. They were marching to the sound of the trumpet in obedience to the words of Jehovah. Faith produces obedience. Obedience produces discipline. Discipline produces patience. Victory is a result of these attributes working together.

Israel's obedience to the commands of the Lord was the exact response that God desired. Their faith in Jehovah produced obedience to His Word. Doing everything God's way meant discipline and patience would be cultivated in their lives. What a contrast this generation was to the generation that came out of Egypt!

Important Lessons

There are numerous principals realized in this sixth chapter of Joshua and outlined in the last three chapters. These principles, if we understand them and choose to govern our lives by their truths, will lead us to our divine inheritance while here on earth. Let us look at a brief overview in the closing of this chapter:

• When God has a divine purpose to fulfill, there is no wall or obstacle too high or too strong that cannot be overcome. If God is for us, who can be against us?
• We must keep His Word in front of us at all times and follow the direction of His glorious presence.
• Faith calls for us to march and shout before we see the victory!
• A promise from God does not nullify our responsibility.
• God uses ways and means which may seem senseless to our carnal minds, so that no flesh can glory in the victory that He has obtained.
• As James says, we must be swift to hear and slow to speak.
• Discipline and patience must be developed in us so that we do not hurry the development of our spiritual growth, thus delaying what He sees for us!
• We cannot murmur and complain against God's people, or His ministers. His divine presence will depart and victory will be replaced with judgment.

We can choose life or death. God gave us the privilege of choosing to obey His truth or to live life our way. Joshua made this proclamation, "As for me and my house, we will serve the Lord." He knew the only way is God's way. The only peace is the peace of God. The only joy comes from His strength.

I am so thankful for the Word of God. I call it His

mercy gift to us. He didn't have to anoint anyone to write these principles of truth for our understanding, but He did. Now, all that we have to do is to make the decision to follow Him and His commands, no matter what it looks like it may cost us.

Do the victories outnumber the struggles? Does the joy outweigh the pain? Take a moment to examine your heart. Are there negative attitudes that you have allowed to settle into your thought patterns that control your actions? God has given us a divine pattern to follow in our life. His grace leads the way. Who is leading you? It could be time to make some changes.

It is time to move into a new season. It is time to go from glory to glory. We have to be willing to allow change and meet the challenges head on. He wants to conform us to His likeness. He will use every situation that we face. It is never too late to follow His lead!

CHAPTER ELEVEN

ENDURANCE

Some years ago, the slogan, "What Would Jesus Do," became very popular. The initials, W.W.J.D. appeared on bracelets, shirts, notebooks, Bibles, and anything else marketable. The initials were meant to remind us to ask ourselves what Jesus would do if He were in the situation we were in. It was a creative strategy to cause you to stop and think before acting.

One Sunday morning I was sitting in our church service, and everywhere I looked somebody had this bracelet on. I wondered, "Will we ever reach a level of maturity where we don't have to ask or even question what Jesus would do? Can we know Him that deeply? Will there be a people who will walk in holiness and submission?"

From deep inside my spirit I heard, "Yes, I am now preparing a people who will love and desire Me with their whole heart. They will not wonder what I would do. They will do what I do, without hesitation. Clothed in humility, armed with My power, and reflecting My holiness, they will go forth in My name. This is My Bride. This is my Body. It will be!" With that I wanted to scream out what He had just said to me. I kept silent, but my heart was racing.

Endurance

Every day we face right and wrong choices. The depth of our relationship with Him will determine what choice we make. Do we choose to satisfy a fleshly desire of instant pleasure with eternal consequence, or stand strong in the face of temptation and obey at any cost?

There are two analogies given in the Word depicting living the Christian life. Paul describes running in a race and enduring hardship as a soldier. We have a race to run. It is not the one who runs the fastest, but the one who endures to the end who will be saved. All races have rules to follow. We may cross the finish line first, but if we do not obey the rules, we will not be victorious. We will lose out on our divine inheritance.

You therefore must endure hardship as a good soldier of Jesus Christ. No one engaged in warfare entangles himself with the affairs of this life, that he may please Him who enlisted him as a soldier. And also if anyone competes in athletics, he is not crowned unless he competes according to the rules (2 Timothy 2:3-5).

Both passages emphasize the significance of obedience and endurance. Many people want their eternal home to be heaven. To obtain the prize, we must follow the rules, no matter what it costs. David said that when he became man, he put away childish things. It is time for us to grow up and make right choices. The opposite will result in our destruction.

There is a way that seems right to a man, but its end is the way of death (Proverbs 14:12).

Choosing Wrong

Joshua 6 ends with victory. The Lord was with Joshua, and he was known throughout all the land. The Lord had given the Israelites the city of Jericho. The fame of the Jordan River crossing and the destruction of Jericho, had elevated Joshua in the eyes of all people.

In Joshua 7, the story takes a turn. To this point Israel had walked in steady obedience, but now the scene changes. Chapter seven brings us a picture of their utter defeat. What caused Israel to suffer at the hands of a seemingly weaker enemy than Jericho?

Joshua was being praised by all men everywhere, but now he and the whole nation are brought to shame. God laid out the rules for them to follow, to secure victory. But one man decided to gather to himself what was forbidden, and this act brought the whole nation under judgment! He did not take the rules that God had given to Joshua seriously!

The wall had just fallen, and Achan raced ahead of the others. He searched for the enemy, making sure that none were left to hurt his people. He ran into a half-standing building, and lying in the floor, there was a wedge of gold. He picked it up and saw there was not a blemish on it. It was solid gold and had great monetary value. Turning around he saw a beautiful garment and 200 pieces of silver. He had stumbled upon a small fortune, and his heart began to long for the forbidden.

He remembered the word of the Lord: "But all the

silver and gold, and vessels of bronze and iron are set apart to the Lord; they shall come into the treasury of the Lord" (Joshua 6:19). It was at this moment that Achan was faced with the choice to obey or to disobey.

No one was around. No one would see. He wanted these things and decided to hide them in a place where no one would ever find them. After a few minutes, he checked to see if anyone was watching and put the gold and silver under his garments. When he arrived at his tent, he buried his treasure deep.

Running back to Jericho to join his brothers in the conquest, he smiled as he thought of his buried treasure! He didn't realize that God's blessings upon all of Israel were now turned to God's curse because of his actions. Although only one man had disobeyed, the curse would fall upon the entire congregation.

Because of this disobedience, God lifted His protective hand from Israel, and He withdrew Himself from their presence. Sin will always separate God from His people. They were left to fight on their own, which resulted in their resounding defeat.

Jericho had been feared by all other towns of the area because of its seemingly impenetrable fortress, but the town of Ai was much smaller and weaker. Imagine the Israelites' shame when they were unable to overpower the city of Ai.

God had promised He would drive out all their enemies but because of Achan's sin he permitted the enemy to overpower Israel. Notice that He does not say, "one man," but, He says, "the children of Israel" committed a trespass." One man's sin brought judgment upon all the people. God saw Israel as a corporate unit. If one sinned, then all had sinned, and all would be judged!

"A little leaven, leavens the whole lump" (Galatians 5:9). Take note of the words, "a little leaven." Leaven is pictured as sin in the Word. In Exodus 12, during the seven days of Passover, no leaven was permitted in Jewish homes. Leaven is anything which infiltrates whatever it is mixed with. Having no leaven during Passover made a statement of purity during the celebration. The yeast of sin will spread, if left unchecked. That is why we are told to check for even a small amount of leaven because it can corrupt the whole.

We are not just responsible for ourselves, but, we are responsible for our families, our churches, and like Achan, our nation. What we choose to do, whether right or wrong, will affect the body to which we belong. A small place of impurity will affect the entire congregation, and the results can be harmful. "one member suffers, all members suffer with it" (1 Corinthians 12:25).

Secret Sins

I am sure that Achan believed no one would ever find out what he had done. He probably thought, "I will take these few things and hide them in my tent. What they don't know can't hurt them." He forgot that God sees everything—the good *and* the bad. "The eyes of the Lord are in every place, keeping watch on the evil and the good" (Proverbs 15:3).

The Lord saw the offense the second it took place. More than that, He saw the evil intent of Achan's heart, before he committed the sin. Israel did not see, therefore they did not know what he had done. We must remember that eventually secret sins will be revealed. If we do not see our need to repent, the Lord will make the sin known, so that there can be repentance and restoration. The most secret actions of an individual are seen by God.

I was raised in a loving, but disciplined atmosphere. Nobody had to tell me that my dad and mom had the authority. When I did wrong, I suffered the consequences; when I did right, peace prevailed! Why does it take us so long, as children and teens, to learn if we do wrong, we suffer? My parents believed in that blessed scripture, "Spare the rod, and spoil the child." Believe me; neither my brothers nor I were spoiled!

At a very young age, I learned not to search for my Christmas presents and especially not to play with them. One day my younger brother and I were at home. My parents left us with a sitter and went to visit a church member. It was the Christmas season, and the presents under the tree were too much for me. One by one I would pick them up and shake them, trying to find out what was inside.

I knew that Mom always hid big gifts somewhere in the house. One day, I innocently went into the utility room and looked in the closet. After rummaging through all the stuff, I saw two bicycles—one for me, and one for my brother. I yelled for my brother, and he came running. I showed him the bikes and talked him into taking them outside, and riding them once up the road. Dad and Mom were gone and wouldn't know the difference. We planned to get them back into the closet before they arrived home.

We took them outside and rode our new bikes to the end of the street. Proud of our sneaky accomplishments, we turned around to ride back home. It was time to put the bicycles in their secret hideaway. Just as we were approaching our driveway, I felt really strange. I turned around, and to my utter disbelief, Dad and Mom were right behind me! My heart sank. Fear gripped every fiber of my being.

There was no excuse. We had done wrong, and we were caught! Of course we had to suffer the consequences. This was a big life lesson. I would never hunt for my Christmas gifts again. My famous statement was this, "I can't do anything; I always get caught." If no one else sees, God does.

When was a teenager, I didn't like that. Now I realize that God was protecting me from a lifetime of pain and sorrow. He always allowed me to get caught. My parents would discipline me, and the discipline produced brokenness. This process of brokenness produced willingness to obedience and submission. I learned that character is doing the right thing, whether you are in a crowd or by yourself. There is no such thing as hidden sin. God sees the most secret actions of any individual.

Through the years, I have come to understand a principle, which still guides me today. When I was a child, I would disobey and have to be disciplined. I didn't want to have to suffer, so I would keep myself out of trouble, rather than go through the discipline. As I matured, I didn't have to be disciplined as much as when I was younger. The reason was because I loved and respected my parents and didn't want to hurt them or break their heart because of wrong actions on my part. The special relationship that my parents and I shared held me captive to firm, yet willing obedience.

The relationship that my heavenly Father and I share goes even deeper. I don't want to sin. I don't want to hurt the heart of God. I want to please Him with my life. By His grace I choose to obey. Mature love takes no thought of itself and chooses to please and help others, no matter what it may cost.

It takes more than desire to do good. We are in a war. The war is between the spirit and the flesh. The two are on totally opposite sides, and will always oppose each other.

> *I find then a law, that evil is present with me, the one who wills to do good. For I delight in the law of God according to the inward man. But, I see another law in my members, warring against the law of my mind, and bringing me into captivity to the law of sin which is in my members* (Romans 7:21-23).

It is important to realize that while Israel was marching as an army, they were disciplined and walking in strict obedience. As soon as the walls fell, every person began to break rank, running to take the city and stake their claim! Joshua 6:20 puts it this way, "Every man went his own way!" after the walls fell.

Obedience produces discipline. Lack of discipline produces a self-centered mindset. Our focus moves from concern for the whole, and we begin to care only about ourselves! Submission, obedience, and keeping our eyes on Jesus are three attributes of one who has learned to conquer flesh and walk in the Spirit, to possess our inheritance.

CHAPTER TWELVE

PRIDE AND PRESUMPTION

When God gives us victory over a powerful bondage, we must be careful to remember that it was not through our strength but His strength. It was not our power that brought the victory; it was His. Let this story of Joshua's failure serve as a warning to preserve us from personal pride after a God-given success!

Joshua sent two men to spy out Ai, but they returned to Joshua filled with pride! They told Joshua there would be no need to send everyone to fight the battle. Because of the previous success at Jericho, they spoke with foolish presumption. They decided that they belonged to a great nation, and none could stand before them. They looked at Ai and decided that they were easy prey.

Joshua accepted what these two men told him and failed to ask counsel from the Lord. He sent only a part of the army to fight the battle with Ai. When we do not pray concerning a situation in our lives, we fail to have spiritual insight. When we follow the advice and feelings of our flesh, we will have no spiritual discernment or perception.

In the report that the two men brought back, there was not a hint of dependency on the Lord, although it was the Lord who had brought them victory. If we do not stay broken and dependent on God, a glorious victory will be followed by a humiliating defeat, just as happened here! We must beware of pride and presumption which produces devastation.

About 3000 Israelites went up to Ai, presuming that because they had won the battle at Jericho, they would win this one too. That is not what happened. They began to run in terror from the people of Ai. There were 36 men who were killed, and the rest of them ran for their lives. Imagine 3000 men of Israel, running in terror from the enemy.

The grand and glorious victory at Jericho gave way to the shameful and humiliating defeat at Ai. This speaks to us that after a time of great success, we need to be on guard. Psalms 2:11 says, "Serve the Lord with fear, and rejoice with trembling."

Joshua and his people had become filled with self-confidence and self-reliance. They trusted more in the need for grace than in the one who gives the grace. As a result, they suffered shameful defeat! In the natural they were greater in number and much stronger than the men of Ai. "I spoke unto thee in thy prosperity, but, thou saidest (by thy self-sufficient attitude), I will not hear" (Jeremiah 12:21).

To regard Ai as weak was a fatal mistake. God left Israel to their own wisdom and power when Achan sinned, which resulted in utter disaster.

While the victory of Jericho is written for our instruction to build our courage and faith, the defeat at Ai is given to us for a warning. We cannot expect victory if we do not walk in obedience to His Word! Success always comes from God and not from our own strength. We must live in a place of humility and dependency on God.

Joshua's first mistake was that he took fleshly advice, rather than to seek the Lord for direction and counsel. God wanted all of the people to go and see the victory displayed, but Joshua only sent 3000. Where was the ark of God when they went into battle at Ai? At the crossing of the Jordan River, and during the battle of Jericho, Israel followed the divine pattern every step of the way. They walked in complete obedience to the revealed will of God, fully dependent on Him. The entire congregation took their places and did their part. All were to follow the ark, and all were to march around the wall. God wanted all of them to see His power and glory displayed!

Joshua should have rebuked the pride in these men. He should have discerned the sin that had been committed but he didn't do either. The leaven of Achan's sin was at work, "leavening the whole lump." Joshua did not ask for the Lord's direction, and therefore he did not have spiritual perception.

As soon as these men came back with their report, he should have known that they were not following the divine pattern which God gave to him at Jericho. Deception took the place of discernment!

We will never win one battle apart from God. He alone can conquer our enemies. As long as we are completely submitted to Him, He will fight for us. As long as we maintain entire dependence on Him, we can be assured of victory! Our help comes from the Lord.

Truth Exposed!

Then Joshua tore his clothes, and fell to the earth on his face before the ark of the Lord until evening, he and the elders of Israel; and they put dust on their heads (Joshua 7:6).

Joshua heard of the defeat and saw how the people's hearts became gripped by fear! It was then that he went to the Lord. In his pain and humiliation of defeat, he finally goes to seek the face of God. Such is the pattern with most of us. We wait until a great challenge or defeat occurs to seek the face of the Lord. Joshua should have sought God before he attempted any type of action. I believe if he would have gone to the Lord, he would have been told about the sin of Achan. Because he didn't pray first, he didn't know about the sin and foolishly presumed victory over Ai.

Joshua and the priests stayed before the Ark from morning until evening. Then Joshua began to question the Lord and was worried that now the enemy would overtake them. God's reply was, "Joshua, get up! Israel has sinned!" God proceeded to tell Joshua what had happened. He gave instructions to cleanse and sanctify the people, because He was going to appear in their midst.

So many times we fail to seek the Lord for direction, and then when something goes wrong, we want to blame Him. Whether it is a failed relationship or business, we ask God why He allowed it to happen. God says, "I don't have anything to do with this. You didn't ask for my advice. But, now that you have come to Me, I will tell you what the problem is."

If we allow Him to do so, He will speak to our hearts. He will show us what is inside that has to change. He will use others whom He can trust—pastors, teachers, parents, friends, or spouses—to speak truth. In that moment, we can choose to allow His Word to change us.

Achan sinned by stealing and then tried to hide the sin. We all have done the same thing. Most of the time sin is hidden because of fear and shame. Pride keeps many from confessing their sin, while unbelief in the forgiveness of God is another reason sin is hidden. Whatever the reason, unconfessed sin will bring a curse into our lives, and we will not prosper in anything that we do.

Can you imagine what Achan must have felt? The Israelites went to take the city of Ai and were defeated by a smaller army. What could he have been thinking as he was being chased back down the hillside? Could it be that he knew it was his sin that had put so many in harm's way? If so, how much more hurtful that he still remained silent and did not confess when his friends and comrades were dying around him. Not until Joshua came to him personally and asked him what he had done, did he confess his sin.

Confession is more than telling what we have done. It is accepted as repentance when it comes from the deep groanings of our heart. Without brokenness, mere words are ineffective. There will not be an inward groaning until we realize the depth of our sin and how it is in opposition to the heart and will of our Heavenly Father.

We will not truly be sorry until we realize that our sin hurts the heart of God. Our sin directly opposes His holiness and His purity. Daily we should meditate on the price that He paid so that we could live free from sin.

For godly sorrow produces repentance leading to salvation, not to be regretted; but, the sorrow of the world produces death (2 Corinthians 7:10).

After David sinned with Bathsheba, he tried to hide his sin. Whether pride, fear, shame, or whatever the case, he did not confess his sin. As a result, he not only suffered, but his children after him. One day, Samuel the prophet came to him and confronted him with the sin. David's response was, "I have sinned against the Lord (2 Samuel 12:13).

David saw how he had hurt himself and his family, but the root of his pain was that he realized he had sinned against the Lord. He had hurt the heart of God. When we sin, we not only hurt ourselves and others around us, but we must see that we sin against God, who already suffered so that we do not have to!

When David confessed, Samuel said, "The Lord has put away your sin." How wonderful to know that the second we confess and repent, He forgives us. But we must also understand that what we sow we will also reap.

I heard my father-in-love once say, "We can get angry and punch a hole in the wall. If we repent, we will be forgiven, but we still have to fix the hole in the wall."

Achan sinned and only confessed when confronted. We must confess quickly. When the conviction of the Holy Spirit moves in our hearts, we need to obey and repent. Achan and his entire family were judged and killed that day, and there was a memorial of stones laid over his body. Those stones say to us, "You are never safe in your secret sins." We are never to hurt the people of God.

Every day we are faced with choices. The nature of Christ can fill us so completely that we don't have to wonder what to do, we will know. God is putting a determined heart in the Church. He is putting a fervent heart in His people, who do not and will not faint at the sight of adversity or temptation. They are a people who are not moved by the situations or circumstances, but their focus and their aim is to build His kingdom by obedience to His commands.

When the accursed things are removed from God's people, and the sin is dealt with, He will return His favor towards us. The next verse says, "So the Lord turned the fierceness of His anger from them." When repentance prevails, He stands waiting to lead us into our divine destiny!

Illustration of Truth

As I reflect over the past year, I have watched wrong choices and a lack of repentance bring destruction to the guilty and the innocent. Leaders see things in people's attitudes or character that need to be addressed. Without exception, when these people have been confronted, those who did not want to face the truth become defensive and even angry.

One such person comes to my mind. When our pastor lovingly went to this man with specific counsel, he seemed fine at first with it, but there was no evidence of change. When he was confronted again, he became angry. It wasn't long until he left our church family and blamed everyone else for his troubles.

None of our concerns were without foundation, and what we had feared would happen finally took place. Several lives were torn apart as a result. It did not have to be this way. Instead of his being clothed in humility, he resisted any help. His lack of repentance removed the protective canopy of God from a number of lives, and the enemy came in to destroy him. My heart aches to this day over this kind of person.

In contrast to that situation, I received a phone call from a young lady. She and her husband had come to the altar several months prior, but I could tell that things were not right between them. When I answered the phone, she began to sob. She related to me that she couldn't go any further in her marriage and asked if I could please meet with her.

Later that day, Pastor Mullins and I were waiting in his office for her to appear, and to our surprise both husband and wife walked in. They sat down, both looking so sad. There was so much pain and grief between them. The husband spoke first, saying, "I need help! I have to change!"

I told them it was time to take off the mask and get real. They both began to cry, and for more than an hour they related ongoing problems in their marriage. They admitted that both of them needed to make changes in order to bring healing.

We instructed them and cried with them. As we began to pray, an overwhelming sense of God's presence filled the room. They both asked for forgiveness from the Lord and from each other. They were willing to do whatever it took to change. I said, "The first step is to be willing, and you are! Expect God to move greatly for you!"

Since then they have been faithful to attend church. Things have not been perfect between them, but they are pushing forward to rise from the darkness of the past. They have been faithful to attend accountability sessions, and both continue to display a heart of submission.

What a difference between brokenness and hardness! One brings destruction and the other brings life! God has a plan for each of our lives. When we get into position for Him to use us, He will. We are not waiting on Him; He is waiting on us. Who knows what He has in store for this precious couple!

When we sin, there are consequences if we do not repent. If we hid sin, God will first deal with us privately, but if we do not yield to Him and forsake the sin, He will allow it to be revealed in the open place, so that we will submit to Him.

Even as God's judgment falls, He wants us to reach for His mercy. Look at the example of the thief on the cross beside Jesus. In the presence of the Son of God, he saw himself as he was and asked for mercy. The scripture clearly shows that mercy is what he received. Forgiveness, healing, and restoration are always at the top of God's priority list!

He Is Waiting

As soon as the sin of Achan had been dealt with, the Lord began to speak to Joshua. He told him to go up to Ai. He was saying to him that He had given him the city, and now that the sin issue was destroyed, victory awaited them in the place where they had just suffered shameful defeat.

Contrary to some opinions, God does not keep a record of our sins. When we repent, He forgives. We can pick up our failures and give them to the Lord. He will remake us into a pleasing vessel for His glory and honor. In Jeremiah 18 the nation of Israel had rebelled and turned from the Lord. Their disobedience was displayed in their idolatry and perversion. Jeremiah's heart was broken, and he wondered if there was still hope.

The Lord told Joshua to go down to the Potter's house, and He would speak to him there. Jeremiah obeyed. There he saw the potter remaking a vessel that had been ruined and was without hope. Then the Lord told Joshua, "I will remake Israel if they will come to Me."

The Lord said to Joshua, "Arise from where you are, in the ashes of your sin and failure. Place yourself in the Potter's hands, and He will make you over again!" He is waiting for you. He stands with His arms opened to embrace you in His unfailing, unending love!

CHAPTER THIRTEEN

STEPS TO RESTORATION

A few years ago my husband bought a 1968 SS Camaro. Except that it was an older model, everything looked brand new, both inside and outside. He was very proud of his purchase. No one was permitted to drive the car, unless he was with them.

I remember the first time I drove the car. I thought I was doing a great job shifting the gears, but with every gear change, he was on pins and needles. Putting on the brakes, turning corners, the whole ordeal was quite a challenge. Although I had been driving for years, when I drove that car I felt like a beginner.

I didn't understand, and of course, my feelings were hurt. I didn't want to drive that car again! What I didn't realize is that he had a "collector's item." What looked like an older car with a new paint job was a rare car that was worth more in its restored condition than it was when it was brand new.

He explained to me the interior was original, and someone had worked very hard to get this car to look the way it did. He said, "Diane, this did not just happen. Someone was willing to pay a price and do whatever necessary to restore this car. You see the finished product; you don't see all of the hard work and the process this car and the owner went through. I own a car, which others would love to own. It is very rare, and I want to be very careful not to diminish the value."

I smiled and told him I understood. A time consuming process and a small fortune were responsible for the beauty of its restoration. Someone loved that car and had decided that it didn't matter how much time or what it cost, that Camaro would be brought back to its original state through the patient process of restoration. What I have learned since that time, is that when something is restored, it is worth more than when it first existed. It becomes a rare commodity, and this causes its' value to rise.

My mind began to roam through process of healing and restoration that I had been through. I thought of my husband, and how God had touched his life and restored him. I set out to study and try to understand the process of restoration in our lives.

The Victory at Ai

After God told Joshua why they were defeated at Ai, He instructed Joshua, telling him the steps to take to cleanse the nation and how to deal with the sin of Achan. Joshua had learned by experience to obey every command of the Lord.

He did as the Lord said. Joshua questioned each tribe, then family, and last individuals. Not until Achan was personally confronted did he admit to sin. All of this time, through the defeat of Israel, the death of comrades, and the questioning of each tribe and family,

Achan remained silent. Was it fear and shame or selfish ambition that caused him to keep quiet? Regardless of the reason, he did not come forward. He put his nation and his own family in peril. Sin blinds us until we don't really see those who are hurting around us.

Achan finally admitted his sin, and judgment fell upon him and his family. They were buried, and memorial stones were placed over the graves. The memorial stones were placed there, as a testimony to coming generations, that unrepentant and hidden sin brings the judgment of God.

Divine Assurance

Immediately after the sin was dealt with, the Word says, "So the Lord turned from the fierceness of His anger." Joshua went to seek the face of the Lord; He had learned the lesson well. While he was praying, the Lord said to him, "Do not be afraid, nor be dismayed." The Lord was assuring Joshua that though he had failed, because of his humility and repentance, the Lord would be with him. He was not alone. God was with Joshua and the people. He would lead them to victory

The love and forgiveness of our Lord exceeds anything our finite minds can comprehend. Israel had been defeated because of sin. Their leader had failed to approach the battle of Ai with the direction of the Lord. That in itself was sin. Before we take one step, to move in any direction, we must seek the face of the Lord for His counsel and plans.

The grace of God is evident in this passage. Joshua turned to seek the Lord, and the Lord spoke to him. He

gave directions for the victory over Ai. Fellowship with
the Lord was restored.

Divine Direction

The assurance of the Lord was followed by the
words, "Take all of the people of war with thee, and
arise, go up to Ai." Joshua and the Israelites received
definite directions from the Lord. They were now to
arise from His throne of mercy and go out to battle.
They knew that if they went, obeying every word, they
could rest in the victory of the Lord.

As believers today, we are to spend time in His presence, seeking His face, through intercession and worship, but then we must rise and go out into the
battlefield of this world and take His love to all who have
not yet believed. We cannot neglect His presence, but we
also must not neglect those around us who are in darkness. We have a work to do, but we cannot do it without
His guidance. God is calling His people to a higher level
of worship and a deeper pledge to service.

Unity in the body of Christ is required to victori-
ously meet the challenges that are ahead of us. The
people were not to fear, and they could walk in confidence and faith, knowing that they had His favor, and He
would lead them again to victory!

"See I have given into your hand the King of Ai, his
people, his city, and his land" were similar words to the
ones God spoke to Joshua concerning Jericho. He was
not saying "I will," but "I have given." He was speaking
"those things that are not as though they were"
(Romans 4:17).

God had spoken to Abraham, "I have made you a Father of many nations." Here God said to Joshua that He had already given them the land. Though we don't see it with our natural eyes, we are to look beyond that realm into the realm of the spirit and see by faith that God has given the victory. He is speaking more than a statement of faith; He is speaking as a statement of "divine purpose."

No matter what things look like around us, even though the challenge before us looks greater than our ability, we need to trust in the Lord. We must not look with our natural sight, but with the eyes of faith through the spirit. If we walk in obedience to what the Lord has said with a repentant attitude, we can rest that He is leading us into our divine purpose. No matter what obstacle presents itself, the victory awaits us. We need to rust Him and rest!

Divine Method

The Lord told them they needed to treat the King of Ai as they had treated Jericho, with one difference. In Jericho, they were forbidden to take any spoils. Here, after the defeat of Ai, they could take the spoil and the cattle for themselves.

They would not be encircling the town seven times as they did in Jericho. There was another way which God commanded. Jericho had been taken by a complete miracle of the Lord to teach the people dependence on Him and to give Him the glory for all of their successes. This time, however, they would win this battle through diligence, self denial, and using all of their powers, both mind and body.

117

Remember when the spies went to Ai, they came back with a report of pride and presumption, and they decided to take only a few men to fight the battle. As we have seen, they failed miserably and shamefully. Now God told them to take all of the people. To counteract the pride factor, God commanded a much more humbling method to take Ai.

The strong city of Jericho was won in public, by marching in obedience for seven days. Here, the smaller, weaker town would be won by a hidden ambush—a secret attack from the rear. Joshua and the people had learned not to question, only obey, so the next morning, they went out to war against Ai.

God had already announced that He had given them the city. Why then did they have to go to battle? Why must they put themselves in harm's way? Unless God gives the victory, we will not have it. The Israelites were called upon to be faithful to their responsibilities. God's promises do not encourage laziness, but urge us to obey His commands. Because victory is surely promised in the end, we as soldiers of the Lord are called on to fight the "good fight of faith." The assurance of victory is our incentive from which we draw energy!

Therefore, while Israel was to exercise faith in divine success, they were required to live in strict obedience to the method which God had given. Joshua gave definite commands to the 30,000 men who were to take the city from the rear.

Joshua 8:4 says, "Ye shall lie in wait against the city, behind the city: go not very far from the city, but be ye all ready." They were told where to go and what to do.

The commands that the Lord gives us for spiritual warfare along with our strict obedience to them, will determine our victory.

> *Be strong in the Lord, and the power of His might. Put on the whole armor of God that ye may be able to stand against the wiles of the devil* (Ephesians 6:10-11).

In verse 12 He repeats, "Wherefore take unto you the whole armor of God that you may be able to stand in the evil day, and having overcome all, to stand." God has provided the armor, but, we must "take unto us" and "put on" the whole armor.

We cannot fight battles on our own. We must put on the armor of God. The armor, which He has given us, is prayer, the Word of God, praise, worship, intercession, speaking truth, repentance, faith, the blood of Jesus, and living fellowship with our Lord.

The 30,000 were told to lie in wait, and be ready, be awake, alert, prepared. 1 Peter 5:8-9 tells us to be sober and vigilant, to resist the adversary, and to be steadfast in faith! Can you imagine how humiliating it must have been for their proud flesh to have to turn their backs on the enemy and run! God does have a purpose in all that He does.

In one day, the entire population of Ai were killed. Israel took for themselves the livestock and the spoils. The King of Ai also died on that same day. His body was buried at the entrance of the gate of the city, as a memorial to all who passed by.

The gate of the city was the place of authority. The rulers of the city would sit in the gate and make decisions concerning their city. By burying this evil king in the entrance of the gate, Joshua and all of Israel were making a statement of the power, authority, and provision of Jehovah their God.

After the victory over Ai, Joshua built an altar to the Lord. On this altar he offered burnt offerings and peace offerings. The burnt offerings were all for God. Animals were sacrificed, their blood was drained, and then they were burned to ashes on the altar. This offering represented the total consecrating of self to God.

The peace offerings were also animal sacrifices, but the meat was eaten by the priests and the people. This offering symbolized gratitude and commitment to God. It was also a picture of fellowship with Him.

Joshua renewed the covenant, as he wrote on gathered stones the words of the whole Law of Moses. He then read all of the words, both the blessings and the curses, to all of Israel. Both were vital to the covenant relationship. The people understood that as long as they obeyed, they were blessed. If they disobeyed, they were cursed.

Though Joshua had not followed the divine pattern, and the nation had lost a shameful battle, he immediately fell on his face to seek the Lord. He didn't say everything just exactly right, but when God spoke, he obeyed. As a result, Joshua and the nation of Israel were restored to the Lord's presence and purpose.

Practical Application

Many times we make wrong choices, or wrong decisions. We fail to seek the Lord for His council. He has given us His Word, which is a road map for our lives. How many times do we read His Word to see how to live our lives? When things go wrong, the first thing we want to do is to somehow blame God for allowing us to fail or for things not working out the way we wanted them to.

The key to success in life is obedience to the Word of the Lord. If we do not read His Word and spend time in His presence, how will we know what He says? Everything comes down to disciplining ourselves to do what we know we should do. But our failures, our sins, and our lack of discipline cannot negate the grace of God in our lives.

We will slow down the process of walking in our divine destiny, through disobedience, but when we come to the Lord, broken and repentant, He is willing to forgive and take us on in His divine will. There is shame in falling, but there is much more shame in falling and not choosing to get up and move on!

Joshua and the nation of Israel walked into their divine inheritance, a land flowing with milk and honey, a place of life and fruitfulness. Then they had to make the choice to live every day in obedience to the commands of Jehovah God. Joshua's departing words were, "Choose you this day who you will serve; as for me and my house, we will serve the Lord."

We must walk humbly before the Lord, broken to His divine will. When He brings us through a great trial and

121

delivers us from the hand of the enemy, we must continue to seek His face and give Him all the glory for everything that He does in our lives. He will continue the work He has started in us, if we will just submit to His loving direction.

The Restoration Process

In Exodus 22 we read that if one sheep was stolen, the thief had to give back five more or four oxen. Whatever was stolen was restored in greater number than at the beginning. Job lost everything, but was restored with twice more than he had in the beginning.

Matthew 10:29 tells us that whatever we give up to follow Christ, will be restored to us one hundred fold! We can never lose when serving the Lord. Sometimes it may feel that way, but we need to trust that God is working something more than what we can see with the natural eye.

Jacob's son Joseph was put into a pit by his brothers, and then sold into slavery. He was unjustly accused and was sent to the prison. Everywhere he went, God was teaching him principles that would guide him throughout his life and as he became the redeemer of his family.

He went from the pit, to prison, to the palace! Each step of the way God was in control! We do not read anywhere that Joseph grumbled or complained. He waited on the deliverance of God. He was restored and possessed more than he ever had before!

Restoration means re-establishment, to replace, to return, to revive, to rebuild, or to bring back to life! It doesn't matter how much we have lost and how lifeless it may seem, God wants to bring back life to those places of pain and death. In *Strongs' Concordance*, the Greek meaning of restoration is "recovery of breath, revival, to cool off or relieve, and intensity." Between the decision of judgment and the pledge of restoration, the vital command is to repent!

Repent therefore, and be converted, that your sins may be blotted out, so that times of refreshing may come from the presence of the Lord... (Acts 3:19).

The above passage illustrates the process of restoration. The first step is to repent of sin, then the Lord will send a refreshing of His Spirit. He will recover life to you. Revival will permeate your soul! When we repent, He will send to us an intense awareness of His presence. Just like the 1968 Camaro after restoration that was worth more than it was in its original state, our value will increase. What made its value go up? Someone gave their time and exercised patience, to bring out the beauty.

The process, the hours, the costs, are all unseen. The finished product is what catches the eye of the passerby. What it cost to bring about successful restoration is known only to the restorer who worked on the vehicle. The unseen work done by the owner increases the value.

This is the same with you and me. No one else knows or sees the struggles that bring us to the place of His presence and His purpose. Rest assured God will see you through. Place yourself in the hands of the Creator and submit to His forming hands.

Like Joshua, I say, "I choose to serve the Lord, and submit my whole life into His Hands." No matter what has happened, whether you are the innocent victim of the failure, or you were responsible for the set back, make the choice to repent and get back in His will and purpose for your life!

CHAPTER FOURTEEN

HEALED AND WHOLE

Throughout the pages of this book you have read personal illustrations pertaining to my life and that of my family. I shared this information with you because I want to demonstrate through real life situations that God's Word and His principles do carry us through to success if we will walk in obedience to His commands. We all have challenges to face and trials to walk through. Whether our heavenly Father allows the battle in order to mature us, or if Satan comes at us with temptations to destroy our lives, we can run to the Lord Jesus, and He will love us, wash us, and restore us.

No matter how dark the night or how long the day, He is the deliverer and the restorer of the broken heart. My life has always evolved around the church. My parents were traveling and preaching revivals when I was born. Not long after my birth, my dad, at 19 years of age, accepted his first pastorate.

Seventeen months after my birth, my brother Terry was born. Four years later, my brother Ricky was born. We were all very close. We had the usual sibling spats, but never anything major. My parents would never allow us to hold grudges. We were not even allowed to pout, to get our way. It just didn't work in our family.

In 1965, we moved to Hamilton, Ohio. Dad felt that God was leading us to pastor a church in the area. At the beginning, the church was small, but in no time, we were experiencing a fresh move of the Spirit. The congregation began to outgrow the building so property was purchased to build a new church.

We moved into the new building one Easter. It seemed that Dad had tapped into a stronger anointing and fresh revelation for each service. Mom always sat in the center section, three pews back, and all throughout Dad's preaching, she prayed.

At seventeen, my brother, Terry, became the music director of our church. He was very gifted in singing and playing the piano. The greatest gift was the strength of the anointing that filled his life.

My younger brother, Ricky, played the trumpet in the church band and had his own bus route on Sunday mornings. Many times I would see Rick carry those little children into the church. It didn't matter what they looked like or smelled like, he loved them and they knew it! He also had dreams of becoming a pediatrician. As the anointing on his life increased, Dad was receiving more and more calls to preach conferences and the like. He also went to the mission field twice a year. He had a heart hunger for souls, and for believers to grow and to mature in their walk with Christ. He had the loving care of a genuine shepherd. He and my mother shared one heart of ministry. We were not a perfect family, but, we loved one another, and we loved the place that God had us. We loved the people of Hamilton Christian Center, and our lives were fulfilled.

When I was in my early 20s, and my brother was around 19 years old, I remember one day my dad asked my mom if she thought we would ever leave home and get our own place. Neither of us had a steady dating relationship. Our lives were full going to college, working in the ministry of our church, and we loved home. Why leave? Dad loved us, but he just wondered!

Suddenly one night, October 15, 1977 everything changed! Dad had been invited to preach at his home church. He asked that we all go be with him on Friday night in Kentucky. We were with Dad, encouraging him, as he preached with passion, to the packed congregation.

I looked around and spotted my mom, she was as usual, praying for dad, as he poured out his heart to the people. Terry was on the pulpit, listening intently to every word that was being said. Besides the music ministry, he felt he was called to preach. He had ministered in song just before Dad preached and had prepared their hearts to receive the word. I thought, *God has so anointed and gifted you; there is just no telling what your future holds.*

My brother had just signed a recording and writing contract with Word Music in Nashville. You would never have known it. He was such a young man of integrity; he didn't think to act in pride. I was proud of him. I felt I knew him better than anyone. His bedroom was just across the hall from mine. Many nights I would wake up through the night and notice his light on. Without fail, when I walked into his room to check and see what was going on, he would be lying in his bed, with his Bible laying across his chest, and he would be asleep. I would place his Bible on the stand by his bed, cover him up, and turn out the light, walking out of his room with a smile. I knew his heartbeat!

I looked around for Rick. There he was sitting quietly, listening to every word. We knew better than not to listen. We had failed to listen before, and we knew the consequences! Rick was so handsome. He looked really handsome in his new clothes. He was in a growth spurt, and Mom had just taken him shopping for clothes that fit him. He sat by his pretty little girlfriend. I thought, *I don't ever want any girl to hurt him. I'm going to watch out for him. I know how girls can be.*

I was blessed! My family, though not perfect, was the joy of my life. My parents, especially Dad, had been very strong in discipline. When I was a child, I didn't like it much. Now that I was older, I was thankful!

The service was over. The people had heard the truth of the Word, and the Spirit of the Lord had truly touched all of us. Dad was preaching a message of ruling and reigning in our lives, not allowing circumstances to control us. Lives were changed, and destinies were fixed!

The next morning, Mom went home to Hamilton, Ohio. She was going to prepare food for the special services we were having on Sunday at our church. My brother Terry and I taught a class of 50 teenagers. I decided at 4:00 p.m. to return home with a friend. She just happened to stop by on her way home.

I went back home, but with the reluctance of my dad. He wanted me to stay and be with him, but he understood that one of us needed to be fresh for Sunday morning's class. He walked me out to the car in the rain. I hugged him and told him I loved him. He gently patted my head, and said, "Sissy, I love you." I got into the car. We pulled out. When I looked back, Dad was standing waving goodbye to me. There he stood in the rain, watching until I was out of sight.

My brothers were staying with Dad. They would return, later that night, in our private plane that Dad owned in partnership. Terry stayed to sing and help Dad with the service. Ricky stayed because he wanted to sit by his new girlfriend, one last time.

Later that night, Mom and I were home by ourselves. She was in the kitchen. I was upstairs, in my bedroom, studying for class. I fell asleep around 10:45. Suddenly, the next thing I knew my mom was saying to me, "Diane, Diane, get up! Wake up! The airport has called they have lost your dad's plane on radar!"

Her words began to pierce the fuzziness of my sleep. Did I hear her right? What? This could not be! No way! I jumped out of bed screaming for Mom to repeat what she had said. The telephone rang again. It was another airport that had lost contact. Oh my God, NO! We began to realize that this could be happening.

Mom sat down on the couch, and I sat on the floor in front of her. I laid my head in her lap, saying over and over again, "No, Mom, no, not three, not three at one time." She stroked my head, and said, "Diane, I don't know, I just don't know." We held to each other and sobbed. She asked me to get her a Bible. I asked her which one. She just said to get the closest one.

I picked a Bible from the stereo, close by. There on the front, was Ricky's name printed on it. I told Mom it was his Bible. Somehow it comforted her, for me to read his Bible. She had me read aloud Psalms 23, over and over, until the telephone rang, again. It was friends who had begun to hear. They were coming to be with us.

We went through two painful and excruciating, days and nights, of not knowing where they were, worrying about their exposure to the cold, blustery weather. The wreckage of the plane and my families' bodies were not found until Monday.

My mom held onto Rick's Bible, the whole time. She never let go of it. When it was quiet she would have me, or someone nearby, read it to her. My mother never took any prescribed medication to calm her nerves or to help her to sleep. She trusted in the grace and strength of the Word and the love of her Savior to get her through this devastating time.

On Monday morning, at 8:00, she called me to her and asked me to sit down. She said, "Diane we have to allow God's will to be done. If He wants our family, we must say, not my will, but Yours, oh Lord." At first I didn't want to. I cried and cried on my mom's shoulder. Then, together, we prayed, "Lord, we submit to Your will." It wasn't easy, but we knew we must!

Then Mom addressed the friends who had gathered around us, "I can't take any more of this waiting! I want all of you to agree with me that by noon today, we will receive word that my family has been found." Everyone there—over 100 people—knelt together and agreed in prayer.

The next four hours, I walked from room to room. My heart was breaking. It seemed more than I could bear. Every few minutes I would return to where Mom was. There she would be, clutching my brother's Bible, praying, singing, worshipping, or just sitting quietly.

Through her tears, I heard her softly speak their names, as if she were trying to talk to them or somehow let them know that she was praying for them.

I knew I was hurting more than words could say, and I couldn't imagine losing her husband, and two sons. I joined Mom on the couch. We sat quietly, waiting, hoping, hurting, and not knowing. I heard the telephone ring. I grabbed my mother's hand, and asked her what time it was. It was 12:00 noon. Just then a close friend came into the room. He had answered the telephone. I knew by the look on his face that the news was not what we wanted to hear!

He stood in front of us with tear-filled eyes and pain-filled words and said, "They have found the plane. There are no survivors." I looked at my mom. She began sobbing and speaking their names. She went to her knees. I began to run through the house.

Our three men were everywhere—their pictures, clothes, cars, the piano, Rick's trumpet, even their smell permeated our home. I pulled pictures off the walls, asking everyone, "Why, why did it happen?" I headed for the front door. I couldn't believe this had happened. I wanted to run to escape the pain!

Before I could get through the door, a precious lady from our church stopped me. In a calming voice she said to me, "Diane, your Daddy wouldn't want you to run. He would want you to allow the Word that he has preached all of your life; to work in you, right now. You have a choice to allow that to happen." I knew she was right. Knowing didn't make it easier, but I turned and walked in the living room, to be with my mother.

There she was, lying on the floor, crying, still holding onto Ricky's Bible. I went to her and held her in my arms. We cried together, and at that moment strength came to me, that I had never known before. I knew God was with us. Life had changed, as I knew it. Nothing would ever be the same.

One thing I knew—I would take care of my mother, and my life was not my own. In a moment's time I lost my dad, my brothers, our home, our car, and all our plans and dreams. I was no longer the "pastor's daughter," and that had always been my comfort zone of identity. Dad wouldn't be there to guide me anymore, but what he had invested in me would remain.

The following Tuesday night, I was getting ready to go to the visitation. How could we do it? It would have hurt enough to see one casket, but we had to look at three. I began to feel anger. A close friend was with me. She had flown in from California to stay with us. She and my brother had been dating, and all of us were very close.

She looked at me, knowing something was not right. I sat on the edge of my bed and stared out the window. The pain was unbearable. My heart was broken. She finally asked me what was wrong. I told her I couldn't do it. I didn't understand any of it. I was angry, and I questioned the love of God!

She sat down beside me, allowing me to vent my pain and anger, and then said to me, "Diane, I understand your pain and your anger, but don't be mad at God. You know the Word that your daddy taught you all of your life will get you through this. You have to walk in the Word that you know. You have to let your dad's life reflect through yours, and allow God's love to bring healing. You don't have any hope if you shut God out of your life!"

She was right, and I knew, at that moment, I had a choice to make. I could either walk away from everything I had been taught, or I could walk into this storm, trusting that God would somehow get us through. I knew I had to live and cultivate the word that my dad had planted in me.

We had lost everything dear to us. I wouldn't hear the gentle voice of my dad, telling me he loved me again. My brother would never get on my nerves again, practicing the piano, in the middle of my studying. I wouldn't be able to pick out my little brother's clothes again because he wanted to look good for the girls. We wouldn't throw the ball again in the front yard. There would be no more meal times around the Robinson table. How was life going to be? How could God take such devastation and make me whole again?

We got through the services and faced thousands of people. For two years my mom and I slept together. We didn't want to feel the loneliness. Without fail, I would wake up around 2:00 am, and Mom would not be there. When I went to find her, she was always in the same place—lying on the floor in the living room, with her face down on an open Bible.

Tuesday night, October 18, 1977, is a memorable night in my life. By His grace, I made the choice to follow the Lord and allow Him to grow me into my divine purpose! It has not always been easy, but growing and maturing never is.

I now have a husband and two sons of my own who bear resemblance to my dad and brothers. We are in full time ministry at Calvary Christian Center. I have given my life away to minister to those who are hurting from a broken heart, a stronghold of sin, or whatever their need may be. Like my parents and parents-in-love, I have crossed the line, and my desire is to win the harvest and see those who are born again, mature and grow into His likeness.

I know what God can do when you have lost everything. When there is no hope, He will become your hope. We will not understand everything we are faced with but we need to trust the Lord and give Him the broken pieces of our lives. When we go to Him with a broken and repentant heart, He will put everything back together for us.

Through studying His Word, I have found that when anything is restored, it is always increased, multiplied, or improved, so that its latter state is much better than its original one! My dad and brothers are not here with me, but I have hope that I will see them again. I can laugh again. My mother is the life of any gathering. Today, people who know what we have been through, say to us, "I am amazed at your laughter!"

When God heals us, He does a complete restoration! My mother and I have experienced it. You can, too! What can separate us from the love of God? Nothing!

Who shall separate us from the love of Christ? Shall tribulation, or distress, or persecution, or famine, or nakedness, or peril, or sword? As it is written: "For Your sake we are killed all day long; we are accounted as sheep for the slaughter." Yet in all these things we are more than conquerors through Him who loved us (Romans 8:35-36).

CHAPTER FIFTEEN

A BALANCED HEART

The test of our love for God is found in the desires of our heart. Do we seek His face, or do we seek His hand? Do we long for His *presence*, or His *presents*? What is the longing of your heart? What is your driving passion? Does the fire of your soul drive you closer to the Lord or farther away?

In Psalms 27 David tells us the desire of his heart, "to live in the house of the Lord all of the days of my life, delighting in the Lord's perfections, and meditating in His Temple." The passion of his soul was to continually dwell in the presence of the Lord. He desired to know the Lord so deeply that His holiness became the integral part of who David was, and the deciding factor of all that he did.

In Joshua's farewell speech (chapter 23) to the nation of Israel, He said, "As for me and my house, we will serve the Lord." The Hebrew meaning of the word "serve" is "bond service," and "worshipper." Our relationship with the Lord and our knowledge of Him will deepen to the degree that we understand the principle of service and worship. I believe that the emerging church, of Jesus Christ, will be distinguished by its heart of worship, and unending passion to serve others.

A Faithful Heart

In Exodus 21, the transfer of the name, "servant" to "bondservant," is illustrated for us. God gave His law concerning servants. If a Hebrew servant was bought, he stayed with his master for six years. In the seventh year, he was to be released from service. In the Old Testament, one became a servant when his impoverished parents sold him, when they were kidnapped and then sold into slavery, or when one sold himself into slavery to clear up debts.

The seventh year was considered the slave's year of freedom. The servant had the choice to stay with his master, or he was freed to chase his own dreams. If he stayed, his master would bring him to the doorpost of his home and pierce his ear. This was an outward sign that the servant had been freed, but because of a covenant relationship that had developed between the servant and the master, the servant chose to stay!

This master/servant relationship can represent the relationship between us and the Lord, as we grow and mature, becoming more like our Master. But, the master also represents leaders, and the servants represent the people of God.

Growth and maturity are not pain free; they are full of discomfort. Where did we get the idea that being in God's will is without discomfort? Who told us it would be easy? Can you imagine the hours the servant in Exodus 21 spent working in his master's fields and vineyards? It wasn't his house, his land, his goals, or dreams. He was not his own; he had been paid for. He would do what was required of him. He worked and received wages. Day by day, hour after hour, he remained in the field, faithful to his responsibility. The scorching desert sun beat down upon his back, and sweat ran down his brow. As he wiped his face, the dirt from the field met with the sweat of his brow. Although his eyes burned and his vision dimmed, he kept working. He stayed faithful, even when he was miserable. In the process of time, he would be free, and someone else would work the field, but for now, he stayed in his place.

Day after day the servant went to work. Just as the heat was becoming unbearable, he looked up and there was his master, with a pitcher of water. *How did he know how thirsty I was?* the servant wondered as he drank the cool water. He thanked him and went back to his duties. The next day he looked up and saw his master coming with lunch. This had not happened before. He wondered what was happening.

One day he was called in from the field, and invited to eat at the master's table. As they talked and laughed together, the servant began to see his master in a different light. The time spent together was building a relationship of mutual respect. They were becoming friends. As he rose from the table to go back out to the field, his master put his arm around his servant, and expressed his appreciation and love for all of his hard work. The servant humbly smiled and went back to the field.

In just a few days, his seven year commitment would be over. He would be allowed to take his family and leave. Where would he go? Leaving would mean starting all over again. This was a great job, and he had truly learned to love his master.

As he was coming in from the fields, his master met him and asked him to come into his house and refreshed him with a cool drink of water. His master said, "I have watched you labor faithfully. I have seen your persistence. Whether the strong winds blew, or the hot sun beat down upon your back, you stayed committed to your work. I have watched you thirst for water, but not wanting to leave your place of responsibility, you stayed. Though severely uncomfortable, you remained faithful! As other servants came to work for me, I have seen you gather them to yourself and teach them the best way to produce the most fruit for their labor. Nothing you did, whether small or large, went unseen. You have been steadfast and loyal for seven years. Now it is time for me to release you from your commitment. You are free to go."

Immediately all the experiences, good and bad, of the last six years begin to travel through the servant's mind—the lonely times, away from his family and the days of unending labor with nothing to show for it. His memories took him to the season of the harvest, when crops failed. That year, there was no harvest. He had worked long and hard hours, but there was still no fruit! Surely his master would want him to pay! But no, he was not charged with failure; he was not to blame. He was willing to take the blame, but his master encouraged him to dream of next year and a greater harvest, greater success!

In his heart, he did not want to leave; he wanted to stay and work for his master. It was no longer a job to him. The vineyard felt like his; he knew there was a greater harvest to reap. He had worked so hard and so long in the fields of his master that now his master's dreams, his master's vision of a massive harvest, had become his own.

He turned to his master and said, "Sir, I do not want to leave you. I have given the best of my effort and time to you, and I want to stay with you. Your dreams have become mine! You have been good to me. You have watched over my family and me. I don't want to leave you. We are safe here in your care. We will stay with you."

His master began to weep. As the tears ran down his cheeks, he put his arms around his servant and said, "Nothing would make me happier than for you to stay. What you don't know is that before you came to me, I saw you. I envisioned you as a caretaker of my gardens and my fields. When you arrived, I saw that you had some rough edges that needed to be worked away. I knew deep within you was a faithful, purposeful man of loyalty.

You have been a faithful servant. I am aware of the times you have wanted to run because of the miserable elements, but your loyal heart bid you to stay and work in my fields. You stayed faithful to your duties and went beyond all expectations. I want to promote you. I want you to watch over the others and become the caretaker of my fields.

They embraced and walked together to the porch. There the master pierced a hole through the man's ear. This was a visible mark of the loving relationship between the servant and his master. He was no longer called a servant; his title was changed to "bondservant."

"I stay in your service because I choose to, as a result of the love and respect we share."

The servant runs to his small living quarters. There his wife is waiting for him. She knows he will be tired and hungry. She knows this is the day he will be freed to go where he wants to. Here he comes. What is this? He is running. He is smiling through tears. What has happened? When he walks through the door, he tells his wife, "We are not leaving, we are here forever. I chose to remain with my master. It is here that we will fulfill our purpose. It is here, our lives will be full!"

Rest assured, it was this man's loyalty to his leader, which resulted in promotion! He wasn't concerned with the glory of promotion, but his desire to stay and be faithful in duty, moved him into a higher level of responsibility and authority. As we learn the process of true submission and faithfulness to another, we are in turn remaining faithful to our Lord.

It is sad that there are "upside down" mindsets, but we all have all had them. The majority of people pursue recognition and platforms. They don't want to sweat in the fields. They become impatient when they don't get the results they want. They don't want to stay in the back and make copies or stay home and change diapers.

The reality is that true servants don't have to have titles or glamour, and yet because of their servants' heart, they often enjoy both. God can trust them not to defile themselves, or others, through pride!

So many people don't understand the responsibility and commitment it takes to become a friend of God! They try to attach themselves to someone who has visibility in the church or a successful ministry, as a stepping stone to selfish ambition. They appear to be willing to do anything that needs to be done and will do so for a season, but when it doesn't get them where they want to go, they slip away!

The ministry of a servant leader is not a glamorous one, but, oh the glory that will be revealed when we stand before Him and hear Him say, "Well done." That's the only place it truly matters.

The key to being fruitful and experiencing growth in our lives is in being planted. We must be committed to a local assembly. Paul tells us to be rooted, grounded, and established. Before there is growth and bearing of fruit, there has to be a root that is deep in the earth. The nourishment needed for growth and development comes through the root system. If there are no roots, the plant will live a few hours or days, and then it will die.

We serve the Lord by serving people. He speaks and moves through His Church. Everything He is getting ready to do, in the earth, will come through His Body, His Church. The Lord Jesus is the head, and we are His Body. We cannot function separate from Him or from one another. We are all part of His Body. All of us have been given a part to play in the building of His kingdom.

There is safety in the multitude. One can put a thousand to flight, but two can put ten thousand to flight. In other words, when we, as the body of Christ, begin to truly walk together, serving and doing what we are called to do, the purpose of God will be fulfilled!

A Heart of Worship

God nowhere tells us to give up things, just for

the sake of giving them up. He tells us to give them up for the sake of the only thing worth having—LIFE with Himself! (Oswald Chambers)

The spiritual order of Jesus Christ in our lives is that we take what He has given to us, and we give it back to Him. The heart of worship is that we give everything that He has given us back to Him. The foundation and heart of worship is total surrender. It is the resigning of our will to His will, the resigning of our dreams to His dreams, the giving up of all preconceived ideas and notions, and fully relinquishing our life into His hands.

Worship is more than standing with our hands lifted as tears flow. It is more than a song, more than a melody, and more than an emotion. Worship is our lifestyle. It is living a life of complete trust in our Savior, and His ways, even when we don't understand.

A worshipping heart is the result of an intimate knowledge and understanding of who God is. If one has not worshipped throughout the week, it is probable that his attempt to worship on Sunday will be non-effective. We can sing every word to every song, close our eyes, and look the part, but the fact is that Jesus only receives worship from a broken and submitted heart!

We praise God for what He does. We worship God for Who He is! Therefore, our lack of knowledge of who God is, will limit our worship! Knowing who God is only comes from spending time in His presence and meditating on His Word. If we don't take time for Him, we will never know Him. If we don't know Him, we cannot worship Him

*But the hour is coming, and now is, when the
true worshipers will worship the Father in
spirit and truth; for the Father is seeking such
to worship Him. God is Spirit and those who
worship Him must worship in spirit and truth*
(John 4:23-24).

The Lord began to explain to this woman that it is
not important *where* you worship. What is important is
the attitude of your heart and *who* you worship. The
word "truth," here, denotes "reality, sincerity, accuracy,
integrity, truthfulness, dependability, and good behavior
or respectability" (*Strong's Concordance* #225).

Our worship should not be a learned or mechanical
behavior. Real worship comes from a heart that has ex-
plored the heart of God and cultivated a sincere relationship with Him. Spiritual worship flows from our
spirits. It is not merely human activity, but it is spiritual
activity. The term, "in truth," speaks of the honesty of
the word of God joined with our honesty in a heart of
sincerity. Meaning what we say and being what we say,
leads us to the worship that our Father seeks.

True worship is not about looking or feeling good.
True worship only takes place when our lives are emptied of everything except the Spirit of God.

Examples of True Worship

*and Abraham said to his young men, "Stay here
with the donkey; the lad and I will go yonder
and worship, and we will come back to you*
(Genesis 22:5).

God had called for Abraham to sacrifice his son Isaac. Abraham was told by God to go to a certain mountain and offer his son. The word mountain represents "worship." When the company of travelers came to the base of the mountain, Abraham told the young men, who were with him, to stay there until the two of them returned. He told them that he and his son were going to worship.

Abraham was willing to give his promised son to the Lord, and he called it worship. He made a statement of complete faith and trust when he said that he and the lad would return to them. Worship is giving up of everything dear to you, and trusting the Lord for the outcome.

Then Job arose, tore his robe, and shaved his head; and he fell to the ground and worshipped (Job 1:20).

Job had just lost everything that he possessed. His land, his livestock, his home, his children were taken as a result of the invasion of the enemy. God had allowed this to prove Job's trust and devotion.

After Job was told of his loss, he fell to the ground and worshipped. He turned to God with his sorrow and worshipped! The word worship in both passages means, "To bow down in respect to royalty, give reverence, and to humbly respect (*Strong's*). Job knew that his Lord was creator of all. He was in control, and though he felt all of the pain and emotion of the loss, he worshipped!

Four Ingredients of True Worship

But as for the incense which you shall make, you shall not make any for yourselves, according to its composition. It shall be to you, holy for the Lord (Exodus 30:37).

God commanded Moses to make holy incense to be placed before the Testimony in the Holy of Holies, where God Himself would meet with him. There are four ingredients used in the making this incense. They teach us the spiritual qualities of worship that are a sweet fragrance to Him.

1. *Stacte:* The Hebrew meaning is "to ooze out in drops." This speaks to us of spontaneity. Spontaneous worship comes from a grateful heart. It also symbolizes freedom. True worship is not mechanical; it is not a form or a ritual. Our hearts worship freely in response to His loving presence in our lives.

2. *Onych:* The Hebrew meaning is "to roar" or "to groan." This substance was taken from a shellfish that was found deep in the Red Sea. It was very rare and costly. Worship comes from the deep of our hearts. When God pours His life into us, the anointing will flow from deep inside us.

It will cost us to press into the deep things of God. It will cost us to allow the deep of God to flow out of us in true worship. It will cost our fleshly pride and selfish ambition.

3. *Galbanum:* The Hebrew meaning is "brokenness," "fatty," "rich." It is a gummy resin that has a sweet odor and a bitter taste. Galbanum is the sap that flows from a broken shrub.

If we are going to carry a heavy and rich anointing, our hearts first must be broken and tempered by the Holy Spirit. Lori Wilke calls this the "breaking before the making process" (*The Costly Anointing*).

The blessings of the Lord, it maketh rich, and He addeth no sorrow with it (Proverbs 10:22).

4. *Pure Frankincense:* The Hebrew meaning is "whiteness" which represent purity and holiness or the righteousness of God in Christ Jesus.

Frankincense was taken from a tree that was pierced and left all night so that the sap could run freely. Pure worship must flow from a pure heart. It is during the darkest most painful times of our lives that we learn and grow by allowing a pure heart of worship to flow. True spiritual worship can only come from a pure heart not a complaining one.

True worship is spontaneous and comes from a broken, honest, and pure heart. The Lord commanded Moses not to make this incense for himself. It was to be holy for the Lord. Man cannot touch what belongs to God. Our hearts must become a throne room of worship, a place where He seeks to live and dwell!

A Heart of Integrity

The 1828 *Webster' Dictionary* defines integrity as

wholeness, moral soundness or purity, honesty, upright, truthful, clean, genuine, and not fake. Integrity involves our whole moral character. It also deals with our goodness and honesty in our dealings with all people in every aspect of life.

> *The Lord shall judge the peoples; Judge me, O Lord, according to my righteousness, and according to my integrity* (Psalms 7:8).

The Hebrew meaning of the word "integrity" is completeness, innocence, moral maturity, and simplicity. David wrote this Psalm while fleeing for his life from Saul and his men. He asked the Lord to judge him according to his integrity.

A man or woman of integrity is a man or woman of their word. Truthfulness and honesty is the core of their existence. They can be counted on. They live what they say.

Our words and our actions must beat to the same drum. James 4:10-11 tells us that blessings and cursings cannot come from the same mouth, and bitter and sweet water cannot come forth from the same fountain. What we are inside is defined by the words we speak.

> *Make a tree good and its fruit will be good, or make a tree bad, and its fruit will be bad, for a tree is recognized by its fruit. You brood of vipers, how can you who are evil say anything good? For out of the overflow of the heart the mouth speaks. The good man brings good things*

out of the good stored up in him, and the evil man brings evil things out of the evil stored up in him. But I tell you that men will have to give account on the Day of Judgment for every careless word they have spoken. For by your words you will be acquitted, and by your words you will be condemned (Matthew 12:33-37 NIV).

After Jesus was baptized, He went to the mountainside and sat down to teach the people. He placed major emphasis on the words that we speak. Whatever comes out of our mouth is evidence of what is in our hearts. We can only camouflage the truth for so long. If something is not right on the inside, eventually it will be revealed by what we say.

People of integrity do not speak one thing and do another. In today's society there is a paramount lack of trust in anyone or anything. The reason for the myriad of contracts we must sign is that one's word is not good enough. We must sign our name, sealing our promise. We need to be people of integrity who do not need to sign anything to make us keep our promises. The church needs to produce what they say they can produce. The world is watching us more than ever. They have heard too much boasting and not enough producing; therefore they do not trust our words. But I believe this is changing. There is a church, a people who have given their lives to reflect the image of Christ to the world and walk in their divine inheritance.

Let integrity and uprightness preserve me, for I wait for You (Psalms 25:21).

Vindicate me O Lord, for I have walked in my integrity. I have also trusted in the Lord; I shall not slip (Psalms 26:1).

Walking in integrity will keep us safe in time of trouble. Walking in integrity will prove our innocence, when falsely accused. The false charges filed against us will be dropped, because of the proven honesty and purity of our hearts.

And as for me, You have upheld me in my integrity and set me in Your presence forever (Psalms 41:12 AMP).

Our integrity will cause the Lord to keep us in His presence. He will never take His eyes off us.

The integrity of the upright will guide them, but, the perversity of the unfaithful will destroy them (Proverbs 11:3).

Truthfulness and purity will lead us to a successful and fruitful life.

The righteous man walks in his integrity; His children are blessed after him (Proverbs 20:7).

As we walk in integrity, even our children's lives will be blessed. As we train our children in the ways of our God, and they see that we "walk our talk," they will live by the example we show them.

Closing Words

There is a practical and spiritual side to life, and we must stay faithful to that which He calls us to and trust Him to lead us into our eternal inheritance. Like Joshua, we seek His face and pursue His presence. When given the command to take the city, we obey whether we go through Jordan, march around Jericho, or invade Ai. We seek Him, and then we go! Humility, integrity, brokenness, faithfulness, obedience, servanthood, and worship are all key ingredients to walking into our divine inheritance, possessing our land, and becoming all that He has purposed us to be.

It is time to rise up and shine with the glory of the Lord. The world is getting darker and darker. Dangerous days are ahead. There is a glorious Church about to emerge from the shadows. We don't have to be afraid. Our hope and trust are in our risen Lord. He is in control. We must hear His commands and obey every word. Only His way will work. We may not always be comfortable, but in Him, we will always be victorious! It us here, in this place of trust, we can enter into His rest.

References

New King James Version of the Bible
Amplified Bible
The Potter's Touch by Dr. Sam Sasser
1828 Webster's Dictionary
New International Version of the Bible
Strong's Exhaustive Concordance of the Bible
The Costly Anointing by Lori Wilke

CONTACT INFORMATION

To contact the author for speaking engagements:

Diane Robinson Mullins
708 Heritage Drive
Trenton, OH 45067

513-868-3265